Differentiated Instructional Strategies
for Science,
Grades K–8

Differentiated Instructional Strategies
for Science,
Grades K–8

Gayle H. Gregory • Elizabeth Hammerman

CORWIN PRESS
A SAGE Company
Thousand Oaks, CA 91320

For information:

Corwin Press
A SAGE Company
2455 Teller Road
Thousand Oaks, California 91320
www.corwinpress.com

SAGE India Pvt. Ltd.
B 1/I 1 Mohan Cooperative
  Industrial Area
Mathura Road, New Delhi 110 044
India

SAGE Ltd.
1 Oliver's Yard
55 City Road
London EC1Y 1SP
United Kingdom

SAGE Asia-Pacific Pte. Ltd.
33 Pekin Street #02-01
Far East Square
Singapore 048763

Printed in the United States of America.

Library of Congress Cataloging-in-Publication Data

Gregory, Gayle.
Differentiated instructional strategies for science, grades K-8 / Gayle H. Gregory, Elizabeth Hammerman.
    p. cm.
Includes bibliographical references and index.
ISBN 978-1-4129-1650-9 (cloth)
ISBN 978-1-4129-1651-6 (pbk.)
    1. Science—Study and teaching (Elementary) 2. Science—Study and teaching (Middle school) 3. Individualized instruction. I. Hammerman, Elizabeth L. II. Title.

 LB1585.G73 2008
372.3'5044—dc22   2007031658

This book is printed on acid-free paper.

07 08 09 10 11   10 9 8 7 6 5 4 3 2 1

Acquisitions Editor:	Faye Zucker
Editorial Assistant:	Lesley Blake
Production Editor:	Libby Larson
Copy Editor:	Tina Hardy
Typesetter:	C&M Digitals (P) Ltd.
Proofreader:	Sue Irwin
Indexer:	Sylvia Coates
Cover Designer:	Lisa Miller

Contents

Acknowledgments

Corwin Press would like to thank the following reviewers:

Mandy Frantti
Teacher: Physics, Astronomy, Mathematics
NASA Astrophysics Educator Ambassador
Munising Public Schools
Munising, MI

Phyllis Milne, EdD
Associate Director of Curriculum and Student Achievement
York County School Division
Yorktown, VA

Marcia LeCompte
Intermediate Multiage Teacher
Klondike Elementary School
West Lafayette, IN

Susan B. Koba, PhD
Science Education Consultant
Omaha, NE

Angela Becton
Teacher Instructional Support Specialist
Johnston County Schools
Smithfield, NC

About the Authors

 **Gayle H. Gregory** has been a teacher in elementary, middle, and secondary schools. For many years, she taught in schools with extended periods of instructional time (block schedules). She has had extensive districtwide experience as a curriculum consultant and staff development coordinator. She was course director at York University for the Faculty of Education, teaching in the teacher education program. She now consults internationally (Europe, Asia, North and South America, Australia) with teachers, administrators, and staff developers in the areas of brain-compatible learning, block scheduling, emotional intelligence, instructional and assessment practices, cooperative group learning, presentation skills, renewal of secondary schools, enhancing teacher quality, coaching and mentoring, and managing change. She is affiliated with many organizations, including the Association for Supervision and Curriculum Development and the National Staff Development Council, and is the coauthor of *Designing Brain-Compatible Learning* and *Thinking Inside the Block Schedule: Strategies for Teaching in Extended Periods of Time.* She has been featured in *Video Journal of Education*'s edition on "Differentiated Instruction." She is committed to lifelong learning and professional growth for herself and others. She may be contacted by calling (905) 336-6565 or by e-mail: gregorygayle@ netscape.net. Her Web site is http://www3.sympatico.ca/gayle.gregory

Elizabeth Hammerman is a dedicated Science Educator. Her background includes teaching science at the middle school and high school levels and teaching preservice and inservice teachers. As a professor, project director, and workshop facilitator, she has taught K–8 science methods courses for seven universities, codirected grant projects to enhance the quality of K–12 teaching and assessment, served as a Math/Science Consultant for seven counties, and provided professional development for K–8 teachers in hands-on science, effective teaching, standards alignment, and classroom assessment.

She has worked extensively as a consultant, project designer, and presenter for school systems, regional centers, professional organizations, and state offices of education, and has served as an instructional designer for innovative science curriculum and assessment projects. Recent publications *Eight Essentials of Inquiry-Based Science* (2005) and *Becoming a Better Science Teacher: Eight Steps to High Quality and Student Achievement* (2006) were designed as tools to deepen teachers' understandings of standards and standards alignment, and help them meet the demands of implementing inquiry-based science by providing research-based strategies for increasing student achievement.

Her Science Achievement professional development programs for teacher leaders and classroom teachers are individually designed to build leadership capacity and instructional expertise for achieving excellence in science.

Introduction

"The Battle Continues Over Stem Cell Research"

"More of the Mysteries of Saturn Discovered"

"Journal Reports Advancements in Technology and Medicine"

"Scientists Detail and Make Predictions About Climate Changes"

These are just a few of the many headlines and topics that flood the media and point to current and future issues that children will face as citizens in a global community. Preparing students to understand and adapt to a continuously changing scientific and technological world must be a high priority in K–12 education.

Science education is for all students. The expectations for what students should know and be able to do in a cultural context are identified through national and state standards. These expectations include understanding what it means to "do" science, recognizing the historical significance of science achievement and ethics underlying these achievements, and viewing science from the human dimension, that is, understanding the relationships between science and society.

State standards documents provide frameworks for each state's educational system. Formal and informal assessments aligned with state standards provide evidence of student achievement and offer valuable information to guide the teaching and learning process.

Instruction is the collective process through which the messages of the standards "come alive" through rich and meaningful experiences that focus on observation, reason, experimentation, sense making, and reflection. Instruction, to be effective, must engage students and motivate them to seek answers to their questions. Just as students exhibit an array of biological and cultural differences, so, too, classroom instruction must be diverse and include an assortment of methods and strategies to accommodate different ways students learn and know. As such, instruction is a creative process providing students a wide range of learning opportunities enabling them to understand or seek to understand complex subject matter and transfer learning to new problems and contexts. Student interest and motivation are enhanced through active and meaningful learning.

DIFFERENTIATED INSTRUCTION

What is differentiated instruction? Differentiated instruction is an approach to strategic planning of classroom instruction that meets the needs of all students. Differentiated instruction enables students to build a meaningful and accurate knowledge base, develop skills needed to become scientifically and technologically literate, and practice dispositions that are valued in the society. Differentiated instruction requires carefully designed lessons that align with important goals and standards and include a variety of methods and strategies to meet the needs of students.

Why do we use it? The classroom is viewed as a community of learners where teachers and students share responsibility for learning and work collaboratively to construct knowledge, develop skills, and practice dispositions. Differentiated instruction allows students to be physically and mentally involved in creating personal and meaningful learning and enables teachers to facilitate and guide the learning process to better meet the needs, interests, and ability levels of students.

What does it look like? An "environment of active learning" would best describe the differentiated classroom. Instruction focused on important goals and standards may be designed around assessment feedback and student needs, readiness for learning, learning profiles (ways of learning and knowing), and cultural contexts.

Instruction may involve the total group or be designed to enable small groups and individuals to work in varied ways to learn important concepts and skills. The teacher's role is that of facilitator—monitoring and guiding instruction, interacting with students, and mediating learning.

TEACHING MATTERS

Recent research emphasizes the importance of high quality classroom instruction for increasing student achievement in mathematics and science.

1. A study by Educational Testing Service found that while teacher inputs, professional development, and classroom practices all influence student achievement, the greatest role is played by classroom practices (Wenglinsky, 2000).

The study showed a positive correlation between teacher quality and higher student achievement in both math and science, and pointed to the need to improve classroom aspects of teacher quality. For example, teachers need to convey higher order thinking, engage students in active learning, and use assessment data to monitor student progress.

2. A study of K–12 mathematics and science education in the United States identified indicators of effective lessons and used these criteria to assess instruction in 350 math and science classrooms. In this study, exemplary instruction was defined in these ways:

- Instruction is purposeful and all students are highly engaged most or all of the time in meaningful work (e.g., investigations, teacher presentations, discussions with each other or the teacher, purposeful reading).
- The lesson is well-designed and artfully implemented, with flexibility and responsiveness to students' needs and interests.
- Instruction is highly likely to enhance most students' understanding of the discipline and to develop their capacity to successfully "do" mathematics or science (Weiss, 2003).

Clarifying Instructional Goals

In *Science for All Americans*, the American Association for the Advancement of Science recommends that all students leave school with an awareness of what the scientific endeavor is and how it relates to their culture and their lives (American Association for the Advancement of Science, 1989).

The National Science Education Standards offers four goals for school science that relate to the cultural context, as well. The goals are designed to enable students to do the following:

- Experience the richness and excitement of knowing about and understanding the natural world.
- Use appropriate scientific processes and principles in making personal decisions.
- Engage intelligently in public discourse and debate about matters of scientific and technological concern.

- Increase their economic productivity in their careers through the use of the knowledge, understanding, and skills of the scientifically literate person (National Research Council, 1996, p. 13). In traditional science programs, emphasis is given to concepts and principles of life, earth/space, and physical science, with little attention given to the other content standards: unifying concepts and processes, science as inquiry, science and technology, science in personal and social perspectives, and history and nature of science.

Courses steeped in expository methods do not promote the development of critical and creative thinking, problem solving, and decision making. More recently, brain research, advancements in technology, awareness of differences in learning styles, and theories related to intelligence have focused on the importance of providing varied pathways to learning and making science relevant by applying it to the lives of students and the technological world in which they live. Through a climate of active engagement and risk taking that promotes thinking and problem solving, students are more likely to acquire the knowledge and develop the skills they need to be successful throughout their lives.

DIFFERENTIATED INSTRUCTION IN ACTION

The goals of science education can be achieved only through carefully crafted instructional programs that are aligned with standards and goals and facilitated by teachers who have the knowledge, flexibility, and resources to accommodate the varying needs and interests of a diverse population of students. The purpose of this book is to provide a model for planning, organizing, and facilitating high quality instruction based on the eight National Science Education content standards to meet the needs of learners. It is not possible to address the full range of standards in the examples provided in the text, but efforts are made to emphasize the importance of addressing all of them throughout the K–8 science program.

The planning guide found on Figure 3 in Chapter 1 was designed from the model for instruction from *Differentiated Instructional Strategies: One Size Doesn't Fit All* (Gregory & Chapman, 2007) and the model for high quality instruction in science from *Becoming a Better Science Teacher: Eight Steps to High Quality Instruction and Student Achievement* (Hammerman, 2006a). The planning guide provides a framework for instructional design that enables teachers to carefully consider each step in the instructional sequence and make decisions regarding the use of the many strategies for differentiating instruction to accommodate the needs, interests, and ability levels of their students.

Selecting a variety of appropriate methods and strategies for student engagement and success is the key to promoting student achievement. Flexibility throughout the instructional process is critical as assessments of student progress may require changes, modifications, or additions to the original plan.

Figure 1 identifies the topics around which each of the chapters in this book was developed. Information, resources, methods, and strategies are offered to enable teachers to use the planning guide to create student-centered instruction that addresses standards in ways that accommodate the needs of a variety of learners.

Figure 1 Understandings, Tools, and Strategies for Differentiating Instruction in Science

Creating a Climate for Differentiated Instruction	Scientific and Technological Literacy for the 21st Century	Knowing the Learner	Methods and Effective Practices for Increasing Student Achievement	Strategies for Activating and Engaging	Strategies for Acquiring and Exploring	Strategies for Explaining, Applying, and Creating Meaning	Strategies for Elaborating and Extending Learning	Strategies for Assessing and Evaluating Learning
A Climate for Learning A Safe and Enriched Environment Natural Learning Systems • Emotional Learning System • Social Learning System • Physical Learning System • Cognitive Learning System • Reflective Learning System A Planning Guide for Differentiated Instruction Phases of the Planning Model	Scientific Literacy Science Education Standards Unifying Concepts and Processes Process and Thinking Skills in K–8 Science Dispositions That Underlie Science Dimensions of Learning Technological Literacy Integration of Information and Communication Technology (ICT)	Multicultural Education Multicultural Education in Science Gender Equity and Gender Equity in Science Learning Modalities Learning and Thinking Styles Models of Learning and Thinking Styles Gardner's Theory of MI Intelligences Linked to Science Sternberg's View of Intelligence Properties of Earth Materials Aligned With Multiple Intelligences Strategies for Presssessment	Methods for Teaching and Learning Science The Roles of Teachers and Students in Methods Research-Based Effective Practices Strategies Linked to Brain Research and Classroom Practices • Science Notebooks • Lab Reports • Grouping • Cooperative Learning • Adjustable Assignments • Curriculum Compacting	Strategies for Engagement • K-W-L Charts • Discrepant Events • School Site Investigations Informal Learning Environments • Video Clips • Guest Speakers • Displays • Literature • Case Studies	Inquiry Defined Traditional Versus Inquiry-Based Classroom Factors That Support Inquiry and DI in Science Problem-Based Learning Projects, Products, and Presentations • Booklets, Posters, and Brochures • Science Fair Projects Stations Centers Choice Boards Contracts Computer-Based Technologies for Learning	Group Discussion • Questions for Thinking and Problem-Solving Nonlinguistic Representations • Charts • Data Tables • Graphs Graphic Organizers Four-Corner Organizer	Beyond the Basics Games that Enhance Learning • Cubing • Jigsaw Analogies and Similes	Assessment Toolkit • Observation Checklists • Interviews • Notebook Entries • Teacher-Made Tests • Products and Projects • Performance Tasks • Criterion Referenced Tests and Quizzes Creating Rubrics for Teacher Assessment and Student Self-Assessment • Holistic Rubrics • Generalized Rubrics • Analytic Rubrics Planning: The Key to Success

PART I

Effective Science Education

Science is a way of knowing about ourselves and the world of which we are a part. It is a sense of wonder and a childlike way of knowing paradoxically characterized by integrity, discipline and responsibility. The goal of the enterprise is to provide awareness, understanding, and wisdom for a greater harmony between ourselves and our world.

—Bob Samples, Bill Hammond,
and Bernice McCarthy (1985)

1 Creating a Climate for Differentiated Instruction

A CLIMATE FOR LEARNING

Classrooms vary. Some are dull and lifeless, while others are alive with activity, emotion, discussion, displays of student work, and an abundance of resources. Armed with an innate curiosity about the natural world, children look forward to and embrace science instruction when they are actively involved in uncovering and discovering the mysteries of the natural world. What teachers know and believe about their subject area and the nature of learning determine many of the decisions they make about the structure of their classrooms and what they teach and model.

Science engages students and activates the brain through emotion, excitement, motion, challenge, thought, reflection, and concept development. The classroom climate, as well as the instructional practices that are used, ultimately affect the ways students are motivated to learn,

Juan, a fifth-grade student, is shaking as he "stands ready" for his next class—science. "I have been waiting three years for this activity," he informs his teacher. "My older brother dissected owl pellets when he was in fifth grade, and I am so excited that I will finally get to do it myself."

acquire knowledge, construct knowledge, and develop skills and attitudes. A student-friendly, well equipped classroom provides a rich environment for implementing a variety of creative approaches for learning.

A SAFE AND ENRICHED ENVIRONMENT

A safe environment: Safety should be the first consideration in any classroom. Schools should have written safety plans that are familiar to both teachers and students. Federal and state agencies offer guidelines for safety in schools that identify such things as the following:

- Safe standard operating procedures and housekeeping practices.
- First aid and emergency equipment and use.
- Safe laboratory practices.
- Guidelines for keeping animals in the classroom.
- Chemical procurement, storage, and distribution.
- Guidelines for waste disposal.
- Biological hazards.
- Electrical safety.
- Other safety information relative to the grade span.

Appropriate signs and equipment should be readily available and safety rules should be practiced at all times. Fire and disaster drills should be conducted regularly. Students need to be aware of emergency telephone numbers and exits, evacuation routes, proper response behaviors, and safety equipment, such as first aid kits, eye wash stations, fire extinguishers, and fire blankets. In addition, students should know the procedures for the safe and efficient use of equipment and materials.

A safe and effective environment for science requires responsible conduct on the part of students, cleanliness, and lack of clutter. Students should not eat or drink or put anything into their mouths during a lab unless authorized by the teacher. Some students are allergic to certain foods, such as peanuts. Appropriate safety goggles should be used whenever there is a threat to eyes from projectiles or chemical splashes. Students should be allowed to have input into the policies and procedures that govern their classroom. Parents and students should agree to and sign a "safety contract" prior to student involvement in laboratory activities.

Safety equipment at the elementary and intermediate levels will vary with the types of activities offered. In addition to the guidelines in the safety plan, common sense and an atmosphere of mutual respect, trust, and consideration for others will help ensure success.

Internet Resources Related to Health and Safety

- Occupational Safety and Health Administration: OSHA Laboratory Standard—29 CFR 1910.1450: http://www.osha.gov/
  OSHA's mission is to assure the safety and health of America's workers by setting and enforcing standards; providing training, outreach,

and education; establishing partnerships; and encouraging continual improvement in workplace safety and health.

- The Laboratory Safety Institute: http://www.labsafety.org

  The Laboratory Safety Institute is a nonprofit, international educational organization for health, safety, and environmental affairs. It offers courses, workshops, and materials designed to enable teachers and students to learn to care about their health and safety, learn to identify life's hazards and how to protect themselves, and create a safer and healthier learning and working environment.

- National Science Teachers Association Position Statement: http://www.nsta.org/positionstatement&psid-32

  The site includes the position statement and a list of resources.

An enriched environment: Students need to feel safe and secure as they engage in challenging and meaningful learning experiences. An environment that embraces diversity, eliminates threat, and provides support and encouragement enables students to focus attention on learning. The human brain is affected by factors in the environment. Stressful environments can reduce the students' ability to learn while a stimulating environment promotes neural connections in the brain, which may be a contributing factor for an enhanced learning capacity (Jensen, 1998b; Sylwester, 1995).

Marion Diamond, a noted brain researcher, describes an enriched environment for learning as one that does the following:

- Is free of stress and pressure.
- Provides positive emotional support.
- Ensures a nutritious diet.
- Provides social interactions.
- Presents opportunities for sensory stimulation through active participation in appropriately challenging activities (Diamond & Hobson, 1998).

NATURAL LEARNING SYSTEMS

What are they and why are they important? A climate for learning must respond to human needs for emotional safety, social interactions, cognitive challenge, physical activity, and thoughtful reflection. These needs corresponding to the Brain's Natural Learning Systems (Given, 2002) form the basis for establishing a climate in which students can apply the skills of inquiry to learning standards-related content. The emotional, social, and physical systems are greedy for attention and will not allow the cognitive and reflective systems to function at optimal efficiency if their needs are not met.

Emotional Learning System

It has long been known that negative emotions and social interactions can inhibit academic progress (Rozman, 1998). Students will spend an inordinate amount of attention and energy protecting themselves from ridicule and rejection rather than learning new knowledge and skills. Researchers tell us that we need emotional nourishment from birth (Kessler, 2000; Palmer, 1993), and that a lack of it affects us profusely. It is endorphins and norepinephrine that influences positive emotions and supports learning along with good health and success in life (Pert, 1998). Emotions are both innate and acquired. Surprisingly, peers and siblings have much more impact on learned emotions than do parents: 45% influence from peers versus 5% from parents (Harris, 1998).

When emotional needs such as love and acceptance are met, the brain produces serotonin (a feel-good neurotransmitter). When emotional needs are not met, young people often turn to drugs that obliterate the negative feelings of hunger, fatigue, and depression.

A natural high can result through connectedness and meaningful interactions, interesting learning materials, and attention to students' personal needs and goals. Csikszentmihalyi (1990) referred to the "state of flow," where all systems are focused and challenge and skill level is matched. In this state, all systems are "go" and work together toward optimal learning.

The emotional system flourishes in classrooms and schools where the following takes place:

- Educators and students believe students can learn and be successful.
- Students' hopes and dreams are recognized.
- Teachers make learning relevant to students' lives.
- Teachers provide multiple ways for students to express themselves.
- Teachers continue to challenge students.
- The climate nurtures rather than represses.

Social Learning System

From birth we begin to form relationships with others and our environment to better understand ourselves. There are two social subsystems. One system in place at birth relates to dyadic relationships. The other evolves and deals with group relationships (Harris, 1998). The extent to which we feel part of a group influences our behavior in and out of school. All of us prefer to interact with those whose presence increases brain oxytocin and opioid levels resulting from feelings of comfort, trust, respect, and affection (Panksepp, 1998). Yet often in classrooms, there is no opportunity to develop social interactions that promote trust and connections. We naturally tend to participate in groups so that we feel a kinship that is fostered by group norms and values (Wright, 1994).

A skillful, insightful teacher can capitalize on this knowledge by creating a classroom climate that does the following:

- Includes all learners.
- Honors their hopes and aspirations.
- Provides an enriched environment for authentic learning (Given, 2002).

Physical Learning System

The physical learning system involves active problem-solving challenges. It is often the system that is not utilized enough in classrooms although we know that gifted students (Milgram, Dunn, & Price, 1993) and underachievers (Dunn, 1990) have a preference for active, tactile, and kinesthetic involvement when learning new material.

Those of us who have experienced learners in our classrooms who need to have the physical learning system in the forefront have realized that if we ignore this system, the learners will find a way to "move" to satisfy their needs regardless of our plans. The movement might not have anything to do with the knowledge or skills that have been targeted for learning. So it begs the question: Do we build in opportunities for hands-on, active learning or do we let students find a way of their own to utilize physical systems that may be counterproductive to the learning?

Cognitive Learning System

This is the system that we focus on most often in the classroom and rightly so, as we want students to succeed in learning new knowledge and skills. The cognitive system deals with consciousness, language development, focused attention, and memory. This system also relies on the senses for processing information. Thus good teachers facilitate learning by providing information in a novel way, stimulating the visual, auditory, and tactile senses as well as taste and smell if appropriate. However, as previously noted, the emotional, social, and physical systems seem more greedy for attention, and if their needs are not attended to, students will not be comfortable enough to learn. If all systems are "go," students tend to learn with more ease and with greater retention.

Reflective Learning System

"Reflection is a critical aspect of all sophisticated and higher order thinking and learning" (Caine & Caine, 1991, p. 149). This intelligence includes "thinking strategies, positive attitudes toward investing oneself in good thinking, and metacognition—awareness and management of one's own mind" (Perkins, 1995, p. 234). Damasio (1999) noted that the reflective system involves the interdependence of memory systems, communication systems, reason, attention, emotion, social awareness, physical experiences, and sensory modalities. The reflective system allows us to do the following:

- Analyze situations.
- Examine and react.
- Make plans.
- Guide behaviors toward goals.

This is the system that in the rush to cover the curriculum is often left out of the learning process in the classroom. However, the skills of ongoing reflection and self-examination are key to evolving the self. These metacognitive skills enable students to form a clear image of self and to develop the reflective strategies that lead to self-directed learning and success in life.

Children come to school with an innate curiosity and love of learning. They enjoy learning about themselves and the world around them. Subject matter and interesting approaches to learning that are meaningful to their lives and connected to their personal goals for learning heighten interest and increase motivation to learn.

Learning Systems With Links to National Standards

The National Science Education Standards (NSES) identify a set of teaching standards for science education that relate closely to the five learning systems. Figure 2 shows the learning systems with links to the NSES recommendations for teaching.

Figure 2   Learning Systems With Links to National Science Education Standards (NSES) Teaching Standards

Learning Systems	Recommendations for Teaching and Learning (National Research Council, 1996)
Emotional	Understand and respond to individual student's interests, strengths, experiences, and needs
Social	Provide opportunities for scientific discussion and debate among students; support a classroom community with cooperation, shared responsibility, and respect
Physical	Guide students in active and extended scientific inquiry
Cognitive	Select and adapt curriculum; focus on student understanding and use of scientific knowledge, ideas, and inquiry process; work with other teachers to enhance the science program
Reflective	Continuously assess student understanding; share responsibility for learning

A PLANNING GUIDE FOR DIFFERENTIATED INSTRUCTION

The "quantum leap" between theory and practice begins with planning. Instruction is not a random set of behaviors or a collection of disparate activities intended to familiarize students with a topic. Rather, it is a carefully constructed plan for using a variety of methods and strategies to engage students thoughtfully and actively in meaningful learning of important concepts and skills. As such, instruction should be dynamic and flexible to respond to feedback about both the process and progress of learning and to capitalize on unexpected "teachable moments" as they arise.

Differentiated instruction requires thoughtful planning for success. Two models for instructional design were intertwined to create a multidimensional framework for planning inquiry-based instruction in science. The planning model shown in Figure 3 identifies the phases of the model in the left-hand column that require consideration for planning effective instruction. The phases of the model are consistent with models for high quality instruction (Gregory & Chapman, 2007; Hammerman, 2006a) and with the NSES (National Research Council, 1996) vision for inquiry where reasoning and critical thinking are used to develop concepts, appreciate how knowledge is acquired, understand the history and nature of science, develop skills for lifelong learning, and develop the dispositions underlying science.

The right-hand column provides a list of resources and strategies for differentiating instruction. The planning model provides opportunities for students to personally construct knowledge through active learning by integrating strategies for differentiating instruction with inquiry-based science: "Embedding teaching strategies within an inquiry-based pedagogy can be an effective way to boost student performance in academics, critical thinking, and problem solving" (Jarrett, 1997, p. 2).

PHASES OF THE PLANNING GUIDE

The planning guide provides the framework for the chapters in this book. Each phase of the model plays an important role in the design of high quality, differentiated instruction to maximize student achievement. Phases 1 and 2 of the model emphasize the importance of considering content standards and key concepts, skills, and dispositions on which to base instruction. Phase 3 offers ideas and strategies for understanding learners and selecting a context for meaningful learning. Phases 4–8 integrate components of the 5E's Lesson Plan with resources and strategies for differentiating instruction in science.

Figure 3   A Planning Guide for Differentiated Instruction in Science

Planning Guide for Differentiated Instruction in Science

1. **Content Standards:** What students should know and be able to do: Unifying concepts and processes in science; science as inquiry; life, Earth and space, and physical science; science and technology; science in personal and social perspectives; history and nature of science	**Consider:** National and state standards; scientific literacy
2. **Concepts, Skills, and Dispositions:** Key concepts, process and thinking skills; valued dispositions	**What teachers will do:** Review content and identify concepts that address learning goals and essential questions on which to base activities and experiences
3. **Knowing the Learner:** Preassess; use data to inform methods, quizzes; surveys; strategies, and grouping patterns; consider a variety of approaches to learning	**Consider:** Multiple Intelligences and learning profiles; interest, readiness, gender equity; multiculturalism
4. **Activate and Engage:** create wonder; motivate; generate interest; use novelty; identify inquiry questions	**K-W-L:** discrepant events; poem or story; demonstration; video clip; field trip; speaker; questions; school site; displays
5. **Acquire and Explore:** investigate through inquiry; use varied methods and strategies; offer multiple pathways for learning based on student needs, interests, and learning profiles	First-hand experiences; teacher and student-constructed inquiries; problem-based learning; projects and products; demonstrations; action research; centers; stations; choice boards; role play; debates; compacting; case studies; novel strategies
6. **Explain and Apply Learning; Create Meaning:** Link new learning to prior knowledge; make connections; apply learning and create meaning	Use questions and discussion to reflect on process and data; explain data; support conclusions with data; analyze learning; apply content to technology, society, and lives of students
7. **Elaborate and Extend:** Ask and research new questions; construct inquiries based on questions	Action research; applications to community, state, national, global problems and issues; problem solving; inventions; Internet research; community involvement; reading; videotapes; interviews; compacting
8. **Assess and Evaluate:** Capture evidence of learning to monitor progress and guide instruction; provide opportunities for relearning	Use rubrics for self-assessment; notebook entries, explanations, interviews, teacher-made tests, performance tasks, projects, products, and presentations that provide evidence of learning; portfolio entries show work and progress over time

1. *Content Standards:* The content standards are based on the qualities and characteristics of scientifically literate citizens. The standards are the "end product" of instruction, that is, they describe what students should know and be able to do to understand, relate to, contribute to, and participate successfully in the scientific and technological world in which they live. As such, standards provide the building blocks of knowledge and skills for a K–12 science program.

2. *Concepts, Skills, and Dispositions:* Standards-based concepts, skills, and dispositions provide clear targets for learning. Concepts build from simple to complex as students explore deeper meanings over time. Process skills are the thinking strategies for learning and creating meaning. Process and thinking skills develop as students engage in active learning and discourse. Dispositions are attitudes and actions that are valued by the scientific community.

3. *Knowing the Learner:* Differentiated instruction is student centered, that is, it is designed around variables such as student cultural backgrounds, learning profiles, multiple intelligences, interest, and readiness for learning. Once these factors are realized, it is possible to choose a context for learning that is relevant and meaningful.

4. *Activate and Engage:* Capturing the attention of students and motivating them to learn are two objectives of this phase of instruction. Creative contexts, discrepant events, high impact lesson starters, problems and issues, and the like provide emotional stimuli, create wonder, and motivate students. This phase generates standards-based inquiry (essential) questions.

5. *Acquire and Explore:* A wide range of instructional approaches, activities, and experiences enables students to investigate inquiry questions, explore, learn, and ask new questions. It is here that instruction focuses on what students need to know and be able to do, accommodates student interests and differences, and provides a variety of methods and strategies for learning.

6. *Explain and Apply Learning; Create Meaning:* In this very important phase, students describe and reflect on what they did, the data they collected, and what they learned. It is here that they link new learning to prior knowledge and construct meaning. Questions that promote discussion and dialogue are the cornerstone of this metacognitive phase. Questions that require students to use critical thinking and reasoning enable them to make sense of new knowledge.

7. *Elaborate and Extend:* This phase offers multiple opportunities to apply concepts to the lives of students, to technology, and to the social

world. Students often generate new questions that relate to their lives or to their community. They may express interest in conducting Internet research or engaging in action research to deepen their understanding. Opportunities to elaborate or extend learning should be available through a variety of activities, references, and resources.

8. Assess and Evaluate: Formative assessment is an ongoing process of seeking evidence from a number of sources to inform and to guide learning. Notebook entries, written and verbal explanations, quizzes, projects, products, and presentations are a few ways to assess learning. Self-evaluation tools provide a set of criteria against which students can measure their learning on an ongoing basis.

Valid assessments align with standards and instructional goals and provide important feedback related to learning. Summative evaluations are used to determine what students have learned and are able to do as a result of instruction.

2 Scientific and Technological Literacy for the Twenty-First Century

SCIENTIFIC LITERACY

What is it? The development of scientific literacy is the primary goal of science education and may be defined as what students should know and be able to do to function successfully and address important issues in the natural and technological worlds. Achieving scientific literacy requires more than the acquisition of facts. Rather it requires that learners understand the varied ways that scientists acquire and use data to construct knowledge and make informed decisions that affect public policy that relates to major socioscientific issues.

To adequately prepare students to be informed citizens, science education must focus on the eight categories of content standards, as well as the relationships that exist among science, technology, and society, and the meaning behind these relationships. The scientifically literate citizen may be defined as one who does the following:

- Has a broad range of content knowledge, including an understanding of natural phenomena.
- Uses process and thinking skills and scientific principles in making decisions.

- Is able to engage in discourse and debate about scientific and technological concerns.
- Uses knowledge and skills in his or her career to increase economic productivity (National Research Council, 1996).

What does it look like? Figure 4 identifies some of the ways scientifically literate citizens function in society.

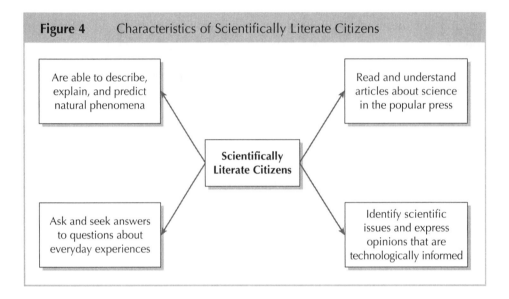

Figure 4 Characteristics of Scientifically Literate Citizens

Are able to describe, explain, and predict natural phenomena

Read and understand articles about science in the popular press

Scientifically Literate Citizens

Ask and seek answers to questions about everyday experiences

Identify scientific issues and express opinions that are technologically informed

SCIENCE EDUCATION STANDARDS

What are science education standards? The National Science Education Standards provide a vision of the scientifically literate citizenry and provide an outline of what students need to know, understand, and be able to do to be scientifically literate at various stages of their K–12 education.

Why do we use them? The standards provide a framework for the development of curriculum leading to the development of scientific literacy. They inform the teaching and learning process by promoting a "hands-on" or "minds-on" approach to understanding the natural and technological worlds in which students live.

What do they look like? There are eight categories of content standards and all are of equal importance for the development of scientific literacy. The content categories provide a holistic view of science that encompasses far more than the understanding of concepts. The content categories are as follows:

- Unifying concepts and processes.
- Science as inquiry.

- Physical science.
- Life science.
- Earth and space science.
- Science and technology.
- Science in personal and social perspectives.
- History and nature of science (National Research Council, 1996).

The eight content categories are described or modeled throughout the chapters of this book to show some of the ways they can be addressed in the K–8 curriculum.

UNIFYING CONCEPTS AND PROCESSES

What are unifying concepts and processes? The unifying concepts and processes are a set of "big ideas" that organize classes of events or objects. These "big ideas" have been developed to explain similar phenomena in the various disciplines of science.

Why do we use them? Unifying concepts and processes provide a way to view natural phenomena in a meaningful way. They provide ways to explain similarities among seemingly unrelated things. Developed over time, the unifying concepts and processes link the disciplines of science and create deeper meaning.

What do they look like? Figure 5 shows the overarching set of unifying concepts and processes from the NSES. The implication is that life, earth and space, and physical science standards are linked to these "big ideas" in ways that unite these seemingly separate science disciplines. Figure 6 shows the content standards for life, earth and space, and physical science standards for Grades K–4 and 5–8. Note that the standards for Grades 5–8 build on those addressed at Grades K–4, providing for the development of content knowledge and deep, meaningful understanding over time.

Recognizing the connections between unifying concepts and processes and content standards can be challenging. For example, if we consider the K–4 standard, "Life Cycles of Organisms," we can identify several connections to the unifying concepts and processes. Life cycles are systems characterized by order and organization; they provide models that explain stages in an organism's development over time; they have consistent form and function.

The content standards provide a basic foundation of awareness and understanding, leading to a deeper development of concepts, skills, and dispositions at the K–8 level.

Figure 5   Unifying Concepts and Processes

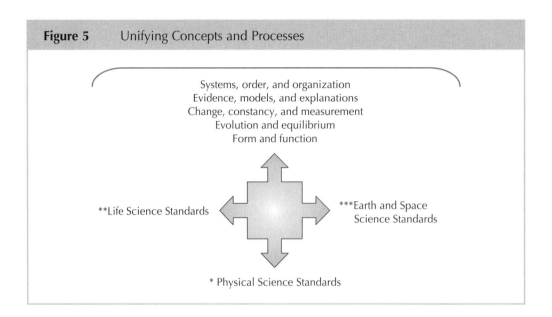

Systems, order, and organization
Evidence, models, and explanations
Change, constancy, and measurement
Evolution and equilibrium
Form and function

**Life Science Standards

***Earth and Space
Science Standards

* Physical Science Standards

Figure 6   Content Standards for Physical, Life, and Earth and Space Science

Standards for Physical, Life, and Earth and Space Science (National Research Council, 1996)	Levels K–4	Levels 5–8
*Physical Science	• Properties of objects and materials • Position and motion of objects • Light, heat, electricity, and magnetism	• Properties and changes of properties in matter • Motion and forces • Transfer of energy
**Life Science	• Characteristics of organisms • Life cycles of organisms • Organisms and environments	• Structure and function in living systems • Reproduction and heredity • Regulation and behavior • Populations and ecosystems • Diversity and adaptations of organisms
***Earth and Space Science	• Properties of earth materials • Objects in the sky • Changes in earth and sky	• Structure of earth system • Earth's history • Earth in the solar system

Scientific literacy can be developed through carefully crafted units and lessons that identify clear targets, are rich with inquiry-based investigations in a variety of contexts, integrate technology, apply learning to the lives of students, and lead students to a greater understanding of the history and nature of science. It is necessary to weave the full range of content standards through the science curriculum to give students the greatest chance to develop scientific literacy.

PROCESS AND THINKING SKILLS IN K–8 SCIENCE

What are they and why do we use them? The process and thinking skills are a set of behaviors and ways of thinking that students use to construct understandings in all of the content categories. They are tools for learning as they engage students both physically and mentally in the learning process.

What do they look like? Figure 7 defines the traditional set of process skills and provides examples of what these skills might look like in the elementary classroom.

DISPOSITIONS THAT UNDERLIE SCIENCE

What are they and why are they important? Another important aspect of scientific literacy is reflected in dispositions or attitudes and perceptions that characterize the working scientist and are valued by the scientific community and society.

What do they look like? Figure 8 identifies and describes valued dispositions. These behaviors shown in the left-hand column exemplify the attitudes and beliefs of scientists and can be modeled by teachers and practiced by students through inquiry-based science. The right-hand column identifies strategies through which dispositions can be reinforced and developed.

DIMENSIONS OF LEARNING

A set of thinking and learning strategies is offered by Robert Marzano (1992) in his Dimensions of Learning model. This model is based on the premise that successful learning is based on five dimensions of thinking that support the integration of concepts, skills, and dispositions for meaningful learning:

- Attitudes and perceptions about learning.
- Acquisition and integration of knowledge.

Figure 7   Process Skills in K–8 Science

Process Skills	Definitions	Examples in K–8 Science
Observation	The use of one or more of the senses to identify properties of objects and natural phenomena	• Using magnifiers and microscopes to identify details of organisms • Watching and recording changes in the appearance of the moon • Listening to and interpreting sound • Touching and describing the texture of natural objects • Identifying properties of matter by taste and smell (with caution)
Classification	A system or method for arranging or distributing objects, events, or information.	• Collecting and organizing data • Serial ordering by properties • Separating objects or organisms into groups based on properties
Making Inferences	Giving explanations for observations; offering tentative conclusions based on logic and reasoning	• Suggesting logical reasons that are not apparent for observations based on sight, sound, smell, taste, or touch • Offering explanations or drawing conclusions based on data
Prediction	Forecasting future events or conditions	• Identifying what might happen in a sequence of events—"What will happen next?" • Making a hypothesis about the relationship between variables in an experiment
Measurement	Making quantitative observations by comparing an object, event, or phenomenon to a conventional or nonconventional standard	• Using nonformal or formal measurement tools to determine mass and weight, linear dimensions, volume, time, and temperature
Using Numbers	Counting; creating categories; applying mathematical rules or formulae to quantities	• Counting objects • Creating subsets of objects • Applying rules for computation • Applying formulae to determine area, volume, or density • Creating charts and graphs using numerical data, such as time and temperature.

Process Skills	Definitions	Examples in K–8 Science
Creating Models	Using two- or three-dimensional representations to show features of objects, organisms, or natural features to communicate ideas or concepts	• Drawing to scale • Using clay, papier-mâché, wood, cardboard, or other materials to create three dimensional representations of animals and plants, planets, systems, atoms, cells, or habitats
Defining Operationally	Naming or defining objects, events, or phenomena on the basis of their functions or identified characteristics	• Describing how something will be used for a specific purpose • Clarifying characteristics of objects or clarifying how a process will be used. For example, crystals may be operationally defined in terms of visible properties and shapes
Identifying Variables	Recognizing factors or events that must be held constant or those that are likely to change under certain conditions	• Knowing and controlling the conditions that need to be held constant in an experiment • Appropriately manipulating the independent variable in an experiment
Formulating Hypotheses	Making statements that are tentative and testable; a special type of prediction that suggests relationships between variables	• Giving an "educated guess" (type of prediction) to describe a possible outcome of an experiment. For example: "Sugar will dissolve more quickly in warm water than in cold water"
Recording and Interpreting Data	Collecting information through writing, drawing, audio or visual display; analyzing information and making sense of information	• Writing descriptions of objects or events • Placing numerical data on a table • Drawing pictures to describe or show events • Reflecting on process and data to discover patterns or changes • Discovering outcomes that lead to conclusions
Drawing Conclusions	Making summary statements that follow logically from data or firsthand experiences	• Analyzing data to determine a level of support for a hypothesis • Using data and relying on evidence to create meaning.

Figure 8   Dispositions

Disposition	Strategies for Developing Dispositions in the Classroom
Curiosity	• Enhance curiosity through inviting and interesting experiences • Offer choices based on interest • Investigate questions
Cooperation	• Provide opportunities for students to work in cooperative groups • Use flexible grouping patterns; use jigsaw; work with partners
Persistence	• Provide opportunities and incentives for students to pursue accuracy and excellence
Honesty and Integrity	• Value and reward honesty and strive for accuracy in work • Maintain a high standard for student work
Open-Mindedness	• Model a willingness to modify beliefs and assumptions based on new information • Establish trust in data
Respect for Life	• Provide appropriate care for living things • Handle living and nonliving organisms with care
Willingness to Suspend Judgment	• Eliminate bias and respect data • Use evidence to support conclusions • Recognize that change occurs over time • Understand that theories change with new information and evidence
Respect for Evidence	• Recognize differences between beliefs and theories based on evidence • Question discrepancies in data

- Extension and refinement of knowledge—reasoning processes include comparing, classifying, abstracting, using inductive and deductive reasoning, supporting construction, and analyzing errors and perspectives.
- Using knowledge meaningfully through decision making, problem solving, invention, experimental inquiry, investigations, and systems analysis.
- Habits of mind—critical thinking, creative thinking, and self-regulated thinking.

Instruction that is rich with sensory input and opportunities to use and develop process and thinking skills and strategies is critical for developing important concepts and principles in science. Students develop deeper understanding when they make sense of what they are experiencing, that is, when they link new knowledge to prior knowledge and create new, more elaborate mental models or ways of knowing.

TECHNOLOGICAL LITERACY

We live in a technological world. The millions of technological innovations, from can openers to solar-powered vehicles and from potato chips to computer chips, have changed the way that we live, work, and play. And technology continues to advance at rapid rates.

The Education Committee of the New York City Council ("Lost in Space," 2004) pointed to a need for sound science education as a means of enabling students to enter the rapidly expanding fields related to information technology and health care:

> Science training will be needed for 8 of the 10 occupational categories projected to have the fastest growth in the New York City region between 2000 and 2010: Computer Systems Administrators, Database Managers, Data Communications Analysts, Medical Assistants, Physical Therapist Aides, Occupational Therapist Aides, Physician Assistants, and Computer Software Engineers. (p. 4)

The advancement of technology is dependent on creativity of thought and design, understanding of materials and resources, model building, functioning, durability, and practicality of products, and the trade-offs (environmental, economic, social, health and hazard, and emotional) associated with the implementation and use of the technology, among other things.

Views of Technology

There are at least four different ways that technology can be perceived by educators and addressed through inquiry-based science. Although not mutually exclusive, these ways are as follows:

● **Technology as computers and other audiovisual equipment—** Radio, television, computers, and the Internet continue to offer a world of resources to teachers and students. Computer software, videotapes, CDs, and DVDs abound in the educational marketplace, bringing with them new learning tools such as probes and digital cameras, information and research, simulations and animations, virtual labs, microscopic and telescopic images, dissections, demonstrations, and standards-based programs that enrich and enhance the learning process.

- **Technology as tools for generating data, organizing, processing, and interpreting data, and graphing**—In the primary grades, students use tools of technology to help them solve problems and learn more about the world around them. Simple pieces of equipment, such as magnifiers, thermometers, balances and mass sets, rulers, measuring cups, and other such items are used by students to extend their senses as they investigate and solve problems. Computer-based programs provide students with innovative ways to practice skills and explore new environments.

At the intermediate and middle grades, the tools and equipment become more sophisticated and enable students to probe much deeper into the natural world. Computer-based tools and programs provide opportunities to collect data with greater accuracy and precision. Calculators, electronic balances, digital recording equipment, computer-based microscopes and projection technology, and multimedia software for simulations and virtual experiments are just a few of the many resources available to enhance learning. Multimedia software offers audio and video explanatory sequences, animated graphics, interactive tasks, slide shows, interactive databases with simulations, and virtual labs and dissections.

- **Technology as concept application**—The applications of science concepts and principles to the technological and social worlds should be an integral part of the instructional plan. For example, following a study of the principles of aerodynamics, including airflow and Bernoulli's principle and forces, such as wind, gravity, lift, and drag, students can be challenged to experiment with cause and effect relationships through the design and testing of gliders, airplanes, or kites for their flying ability.

- **Technology as problem solving and inventions**—Technological solutions to problems that affect society often have trade-offs such as cost, safety, efficiency, or environmental impact. In every community, there are social or environmental problems or issues to investigate. For example, the loss of soil, vegetation, and "green space," changes in the quality of air and water, added traffic and need for roads and other modes of transportation, destruction of animal habitats, loss of predators, decline of open space, and issues related to endangered species are just a few of the environmental problems that accompany increased population and expansion.

INTEGRATION OF INFORMATION AND COMMUNICATION TECHNOLOGY (ICT)

New paradigms for learning in the twenty-first century are emerging that focus on the integration of thinking and problem-solving skills with a standards-based curriculum.

The Partnership for 21st Century Skills advocates for the integration of Information and Communication Technology (ICT) Literacy into K–12 education. The partnership defines ICT literacy as the use of twenty-first century tools to perform learning skills and achieve at higher levels in core academic subjects (www.21stcenturyskills.org).

Figure 9 identifies important learning skills and shows ways that these skills can be developed in the science classroom.

Science educators advocate the integration of skills throughout the disciplines of science. Not surprisingly, models of inquiry that focus on important concepts and principles, process and thinking skills, and dispositions of science include all of the learning skills identified in the ICT literacy map.

Figure 9 Learning Skills Linked to Information and Communication Technology (ICT) Literacy for Science

Learning Skills	ICT Literacy for Science Is Developed When Students:
1. **Information and Media Literacy**	• Access and manage information using a variety of resources • Integrate and create information • Evaluate and analyze information
2. **Communication Skills**	• Understand, manage, and create effective communication in the following ways: (a) using oral communication, (b) using written communication, (c) using multimedia
3. **Critical Thinking and Systems Thinking**	• Exercise sound reasoning • Make complex choices • Understand the interconnections among systems
4. **Problem Identification, Formulation, and Solutions**	• Frame, analyze, and solve problems
5. **Creativity and Intellectual Curiosity**	• Develop, implement, and communicate ideas to others
6. **Interpersonal and Collaborative Skills**	• Demonstrate teamwork and work productively with others • Demonstrate ability to adapt to varied roles and responsibilities • Exercise empathy and respect diverse perspectives
7. **Self-Direction**	• Monitor one's own understanding and learning needs • Locate resources • Transfer learning from one domain to another

3 Knowing the Learner

Teaching expertise is characterized by the degree of efficiency in various knowledge areas including knowledge of the discipline and knowledge of students and how they learn (Gess-Newsome & Lederman, 1999; National Research Council, 2005).

In addition, expert teachers have knowledge of the conceptual barriers that students face in learning about the discipline and knowledge of effective strategies for working with students (National Research Council, 2000). Because students come to our classrooms with a wide variety of backgrounds, cultural experiences, learning profiles, and interests, the more teachers can learn about them, the better able they are to design and modify instruction to meet their needs.

This chapter will identify and describe ways that learners access, use, process, and communicate information as part of the learning process. Cultural diversity and gender differences, as well as thinking and learning styles, intelligences, and life histories influence the ways that students think and learn. Data related to these and other characteristics of students provide valuable insights for the design of student-centered instruction.

MULTICULTURAL EDUCATION

What is it?

> Multicultural education advocates the belief that students and their life histories and experiences should be placed at the center of the teaching and learning process and that pedagogy should occur in a context that is familiar to students and that addresses multiple ways of thinking. ("Multicultural Education," 2003)

The contributions of scientists throughout history from a variety of cultures should be recognized, discussed, applied, and analyzed as part of the K–8 science curriculum. What better way to help students understand the nature of science than to study the pursuits, persistence, accomplishments, and failures of scientists from all over the world and in particular, those from their own culture?

The University of Illinois Urban Health Program offers a list of famous male and female Black and Latino physicians and scientists and describes their accomplishments. For example, electrical engineer and astronaut, Ellen Ochoa (1958–), a Hispanic scientist, has received three patents for developing optical systems used in manufacturing. Dr. Ochoa is a research scientist and a veteran of three NASA space flights. She was the first Hispanic female astronaut.

The National Inventers Hall of Fame inducted George Washington Carver (1864–1943), a Black agricultural chemist, in 1990. During his lifetime he developed crop rotation methods for conserving nutrients in the soil and discovered hundreds of uses for crops, one of which was the peanut, which created new markets for Southern farmers (www.invent.org/hall_of_fame/30.html).

Contributions by scientists can easily be linked to science content. For example, an upper primary or intermediate level activity that uses legumes, such as peanuts or beans, to study the structure and function of seeds, provides an opportunity to recognize the accomplishments and contributions of George Washington Carver.

Why do we use it? The goal of multicultural education is to develop a greater understanding of the complex factors that have contributed to the birth, growth, and development of our nation. The challenge in a multicultural learning environment is to help children understand contemporary views of science while developing an understanding of cultural perspectives that are equally valid and useful and recognizing the contributions of scientists from a variety of cultures.

MULTICULTURAL EDUCATION IN SCIENCE

Multiculturalism can be addressed through the unifying concepts and processes of science, science as inquiry, the content of physical science, life science, earth and space science, science and technology, science in personal and social perspectives, and the history and nature of science.

What does it look like? There are many ways to embrace and celebrate multiculturalism in the classroom through investigations dealing with people, environments, customs, food, literature, and music. Some ways to address multiculturalism in the science classroom are as follows:

- Investigate ways that people from a variety of cultures have made significant contributions to science throughout history.
- Read stories about myths and early interpretations of natural phenomena, such as the apparent movement of the sun across the sky, the patterns of stars, earthquakes and volcanic eruptions, and weather.
- Investigate ways that contemporary views of nature and natural phenomena validate what other cultures have known for thousands of years.
- Trace the history and use of scientific instruments such as microscopes and telescopes in early and contemporary societies.
- Investigate concepts and issues related to science, human health, and technology within one's own country and compare them with similar issues in other countries of interest to students.
- Study natural phenomena such as tsunamis, earthquakes, hurricanes, and volcanic eruptions, and compare their effects on people in their countries and in other countries throughout history.
- Identify human traits and hereditary diseases that are common to various cultures.
- Investigate the foods that are common in various cultures; identify environmental or other factors that linked the foods to the cultures.
- Explore sound through music and musical instruments common to a variety of cultures.
- Investigate the design of fortresses, towers, tepees, mud huts, igloos, and other types of historical and culturally related structures to better understand technological design and the design and construction of contemporary skyscrapers, bridges, and tunnels.

GENDER EQUITY

What is it? "Gender equity means ensuring that all boys and all girls—regardless of age, cultural or ethnic background, or disabilities—have the support they need to become successful science students and feel respected and challenged" (National Science Teachers Association, n.d.).

Why is it important? There has been a continuous flow of research in recent years that informs us that there are still issues related to gender equity that have yet to be resolved in the nation's classrooms. For example, research on classroom interaction patterns and reviews of curriculum materials and participation in extracurricular activities suggest that elementary and secondary school climates are less encouraging for girls than for their male classmates (Bailey, 1993). A study of students in advanced placement (AP) science courses in Dallas (Sanders & Nelson, 2004) found that the number of male and female enrollments in AP mathematics and biology courses were fairly equal, but enrollments in AP physics and computer science were primarily male. This pattern was similar to the enrollments on a national level.

Bailey (1993), reporting on the status of gender equity research, found the following:

- Girls like science, math, and computers, but interest diminishes in adolescence.
- Boys go into careers in science, math, and technology in greater numbers than girls.
- Girls experience a greater decrease in self-esteem than do boys during adolescence.

Some of the factors that contribute to gender equity are related to classroom climate and teacher-student interactions, while others relate more to administrator and teacher-made choices and behaviors. For example, competitive classroom environments as opposed to cooperative learning environments and independent approaches to learning as opposed to cooperative group approaches favor the learning styles of a minority of girls and a majority of white boys (Belenky, Clinchy, Goldberger, & Tarule, 1986).

With regard to technology courses, girls rate themselves significantly lower on computer ability and favor courses in word processing, while boys favor computer science and computer design courses. Another factor contributing to stereotyping is that men are portrayed in more powerful technological positions in print and Internet resources (Knupfer, 1998, cited in Sadker, 1999).

GENDER EQUITY IN SCIENCE

What does it look like? Gender equity is an issue that requires leadership support and participation from all stakeholders within a school system to ensure that all girls and boys achieve scientific literacy.

Numerous suggestions for achieving gender equity are offered by the National Science Teachers Association (NSTA) Board of Directors for science teachers, professional development and teacher preparation programs, the selection of science curriculum, and the assessment and preparation of students for careers in science. The suggestions that relate to the classroom climate and are research supported have implications for differentiated instruction. These two recommendations are as follows:

- Implement varied and effective research-based teaching and assessment strategies that align with the learning styles of all students.
- Ensure that all students are in a learning environment that encourages them to participate fully in class discussions and science activities and investigations.

Suggestions for increasing participation of girls in the science classroom include the following: calling on girls as often as boys, using wait time to encourage greater participation from girls, using gender neutral language, and referring to significant contributions to science made by women scientists (National Science Teachers Association, n.d.).

LEARNING MODALITIES

The Chinese proverb, "I hear and I forget, I see and I remember, I do and I understand," has often been used to support an inquiry-based hands-on approach to learning in science. Dunn and Dunn (1987) classified learners as auditory, visual, tactile, kinesthetic, or tactile and kinesthetic:

- **Auditory learners**—prefer listening to lectures, stories, and songs, and enjoy discussion and engaging in dialogue with other students.
- **Visual learners**—learn from information they see or read; colorful illustrations and pictures, graphs, diagrams, and graphic organizers are useful tools for learning.
- **Tactile learners**—prefer concrete experiences, manipulating materials, and interactions with objects in their environment.
- **Kinesthetic learners**—learn through movement and physical activity.

It takes only brief classroom observation to recognize the needs of young children to be actively involved in their learning. The strategies offered in the planning model for differentiated instruction provide numerous opportunities for students to use and develop all of their senses as tools for learning and to be actively involved in developing concepts, skills, and dispositions.

LEARNING AND THINKING STYLES

What are they? Humans view the world in individual ways that makes sense to them. The human brain is activated through the senses—sight, hearing, touch, taste, and smell—and through abstract symbols. Research shows that humans perceive experience and information differently and process experience and information in different ways. Our perceptions and ways of processing shape how we think, what we know, how we make decisions, and what is important. The brain's ways of perceiving experience and the ways learners approach learning when there is a choice are two variables used to categorize learning styles.

Why do we use them? Understanding the different ways that children interact with and process information enables teachers to better plan instruction and modify teaching so that all students have an opportunity to be successful learners. The various learning style models provide an awareness of differences in mental and physical processes for learning, which aid the teacher in understanding how students develop frames of thought and link these to create meaningful learning. In addition, the models offer guidelines to assist teachers in planning and varying instruction to meet the needs of a diversity of learners. Numerous opportunities to include learning modalities, methods, and strategies that correspond to the various ways students learn are offered in the stages of the planning model.

What do they look like? The many learning and thinking style models differ in the ways they classify learners. The models are generally based to some extent on the ways learners perceive and process information and approach learning. Four learning and thinking models are shown and described. Although the developers take different approaches to their models and use different criteria, there are similarities in the ways of thinking and acting that describe categories of learners.

Kolb's Learning Styles

David Kolb (1984) offered a model of experiential learning activities based on perception and processing. The model identifies four learning styles and provides a framework for planning activities and experiences. The model identifies four dimensions through which learning can take place:

Concrete experience—learning from specific experiences, relating to people, and sensitivity to feelings and people.

Abstract conceptualization—logical analysis of ideas, systematic planning, acting on intellectual understanding of a situation.

Active experimentation—ability to get things done, risk taking, influencing people and events through action.

Reflective observation—careful observation prior to judgment, viewing things from different perspectives, and looking for meaning.

Combining the opposite dimensions results in four quadrants of behavior that characterize four types of learners:

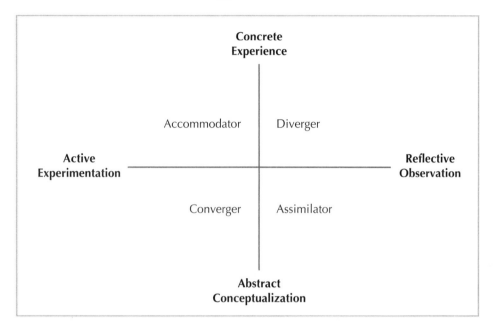

Figure 10 shows Kolb's four learning styles and the characteristics of each type of learner.

Figure 10	Kolb's Learning Styles

Learning Styles	Characteristics of Learners
Type I: Accommodator Concrete Experience and Active Experimentation	Adaptive; intuitive rather than logical; trial and error; relies on others for information; may seem impatient; operates well in technical and practical fields
Type II: Diverger Concrete Experience and Reflective Observation	Imaginative ability; looks at whole rather than parts; people person; emotional; operates well in humanities and liberal arts
Type III: Converger Abstract Conceptualization and Active Experimentation	Deductive; practical application of ideas; likes correct answers; prefers things to people; narrow interests; operates well as a goal setter and systematic planner
Type IV: Assimilator Abstract Conceptualization and Reflective Observation	Creates theoretical models; abstract; little interest in practical use of theories; operates well as a goal setter and systematic planner

McCarthy's 4MAT System

The 4MAT system proposed by Bernice McCarthy offers a cycle of learning that blends both learning modalities and learning styles. The 4MAT system was designed to enable learners to approach problems and experience success from their specific learning style and expand their ways of knowing and thinking by experiencing other approaches to learning.

The model identifies four types of learners:

1. Imaginative learners (innovative) are interested in personal meaning and require a reason for learning; they experience and reflect; teacher is motivator.

2. Analytic learners are interested in facts that lead to conceptual understanding; they reflect and conceptualize; teacher is information provider.

3. Commonsense learners are interested in discovering how things work; they conceptualize and experiment; teacher is facilitator and coach.

4. Dynamic learners are interested in self-discovery, teaching others, and making applications to life; they experience and experiment; teacher is resource and evaluator.

Gregorc's Thinking Styles

A thinking styles model developed by Anthony Gregorc (1982) is based on the way learners view the world (concrete or abstract) and the way they order the world (sequential or random).

Figure 11 shows the four styles of thinking, their characteristics and implications for the classroom.

Similarities may be seen among the categories of learning and thinking styles described in the three previous models. Each of the four categories shown in Figure 12 represents one of the four preferences from the three models offered by psychologists and researchers. The left side of the table shows the relationships between and among the models, and the right side identifies a list of factors related to classroom environment and instruction that enhances learning for each of the categories of learners.

GARDNER'S THEORY OF MULTIPLE INTELLIGENCES

Howard Gardner, a professor of cognition and education at the Harvard Graduate School of Education, professor of psychology at Harvard University, and senior director of Harvard Project Zero, developed a theory of multiple intelligences (MI). Dr. Gardner's theory challenges the existence of a single intelligence and offers a pluralistic view of the human mind. He

Figure 11	Gregorc's Thinking Styles, Characteristics of Learners, and Implications for the Classroom	

Thinking Style	Characteristics of Learners	Implications for the Classroom
Concrete Random	Experimental attitude and behavior; intuitive; divergent thinkers; enjoy finding alternate ways of solving problems	These learners need opportunities to make choices about their learning and how they will demonstrate understanding; they like independent work without teacher intervention; respond to a rich environment
Concrete Sequential	Derive information through hands-on experience; based in the physical world and identify through their senses; prefer concrete materials	These learners require structure, frameworks, timelines, and organization to their learning; they like lecture and teacher-directed activities with step-by-step procedures
Abstract Sequential	Prefer to decode written, verbal, and image symbols; delight in theory and abstract thought; thinking processes are rational, logical, and intellectual	These learners prefer presentations and lectures that have substance and are rational and sequential in nature; defer to authority; low tolerance for distractions
Abstract Random	Live in a world of feelings and emotion; associate the medium with the message; evaluate learning experience as a whole; organize information through sharing and discussing	These learners prefer to receive information in group discussion; gather information and delay reaction; organize material through reflection; cooperative group, partners, learning centers, and stations facilitate learning

identifies eight "naturalistic" ways of knowing, ways that people develop knowledge and skills important to their way of life. "An intelligence entails the ability to solve problems or fashion products that are of consequence in a particular cultural setting or community" (Gardner, 1993, p. 15).

EIGHT INTELLIGENCES LINKED TO SCIENCE

One way of offering diverse learning opportunities for students in the classroom is using Gardner's MI theory to provide choices for the ways students learn concepts, process information, and relate that information to their lives. Figure 13 identifies the eight intelligences and shows their basic characteristics and a few related careers. The right-hand column identifies ways the varied intelligences can be to enhance the development of science concepts and skills.

Figure 12   Learning and Thinking Styles and Implications for Science

Learning and Thinking Styles	Implications for Science Classroom Environments and Instruction
Accommodator, Dynamic Learner, Concrete Random	• Variety of resources and manipulatives • Adaptive environment • Choice of activities • Spontaneity • Extensions to activities • Personal freedom
Converger, Common Sense Learner, Concrete Sequential	• Organization and structure • Clear expectations • Visual directions • Sequential learning • Clear procedures and closure • Consistent routines
Assimilator, Analytical Learner, Abstract Sequential	• Investigative learning • Critical thinking • Verifying information • Analyzing concepts • Deep exploration • Discussions • Reflection
Diverger, Imaginative Learner, Abstract Random	• Comfortable environment • Encouraging atmosphere • Supportive grouping • Safe climate • Respectful and sensitive colleagues and peers • Empathic listeners

Figure 13   Gardner's Eight Intelligences Linked to Science

Intelligence	Characteristics and Careers	Some Ways Intelligences Are Expressed in K–8 Science
Linguistic	Gift of language; ability exhibited in its fullest form by poets and writers (author, poet, journalist, historian)	• Write sentences, short poems, or stories about organisms, natural objects, and events • Write letters and responses to people and organizations related to inquiries • Use nature-related trade books and reference books for accessing information, direct instruction, and extended learning • Trace the history of a scientific theory or principle • Research the lives and achievements of notable scientists

Intelligence	Characteristics and Careers	Some Ways Intelligences Are Expressed in K–8 Science
Logical and Mathematical	Logical, verbal, and mathematical ability; includes "scientific thinking" (computer scientist, meteorologist)	• Include the use of numbers and operations, measurement, and geometry throughout investigations • Explore probability in natural contexts such as genetics, population dynamics, and weather • Incorporate problem solving and reasoning in inquiry-based investigations • Use metric measurement • Collect data, make graphs, and draw conclusions about relationships between and among data
Spatial	Ability to form a mental model of a spatial world; to maneuver and operate using a model (engineer, surgeon, painter, sculptor, architect, photographer)	• Make drawings, illustrations, maps, and diagrams • Create graphs and graphic organizers to show relationships between key concepts • Make three-dimensional models, mobiles, and dioramas • Investigate the intricate structures and functions of organisms and objects • Manipulate materials • Use tools of technology: cameras, robots, computers, microscopes, calculators, and so forth
Musical	Ability to think, create, and perform musically; express thought and emotion through music and rhythm (musician, composer, band leader, singer)	• Investigate the nature of sound and the variables that create sounds in the natural environment • Make and use musical instruments to create sound and learn what effects volume and pitch • Create raps and songs to describe concepts and relationships in nature, such as the transfer of energy, characteristics of ecosystems, the solar system and space • Express thought and feeling through music, dance, and song • Create a song to accompany a science project
Bodily-Kinesthetic	Ability to solve problems or fashion products using one's body (dancer, athlete, designer of clothing or sports equipment)	• Engage in action research • Learn through community involvement • Visit informal science centers, interview a scientist, assist with a science-related community project, invent something, or create, play, and teach an educational game • Learn or demonstrate understanding of concepts or skills through performances, role-play, acting, music, dance, puppet shows, demonstrations, or games

(Continued)

Figure 13 (Continued)

Intelligence	Characteristics and Careers	Some Ways Intelligences Are Expressed in K–8 Science
Interpersonal	Ability to understand people, how they work, what motivates them, how to work collaboratively; is sensitive and caring (salesperson, teacher, clinician, religious leader)	• Assume a variety of roles within heterogeneous groups • Engage in cooperative learning • Engage in role playing activities • Coach a peer or review another's work • Design activities for self and others • Participate in action research with others • Engage in community-based learning
Intrapersonal	Capacity to form an accurate, truthful model of oneself and to use that model to operate effectively; access to one's own life, feelings, and emotions (understanding of self enhances success in many fields)	• Reflect on process and thinking • Set personal goals and design plans for meeting and extending those goals • Demonstrate responsibility • Use self-assessment tools to guide learning • Pursue personal goals and interests
Naturalistic	Expertise in recognition and classification of species; sensitivity to and comfort with nature; persistent curiosity; good perceptual skills (gardener, animal trainer, naturalist)	• Use inquiry to investigate the natural world • Build on interests related to plants and animals, natural objects and events • Ask operational questions and investigate in formal and informal learning environments • Persist in quest for knowledge and understanding • Make natural and photo collections of artifacts and events in nature • Design and make models, visuals, and graphic organizers to explain phenomena

SOURCE: Modified from *Eight Essentials of Inquiry-Based Science*, Hammerman, 2006

MI theory provides an opportunity to view students from a perspective of learning preferences and behaviors. Figure 14 identifies a number of characteristics that define each of the intelligences. Teachers may wish to use this list as a reference for observing student behaviors, for planning instruction, or as the basis for an inventory of instructional preferences.

Figure 14 How Am I Intelligent? A Multiple Intelligences Inventory

VERBAL/LINGUISTIC INTELLIGENCE	INTERPERSONAL INTELLIGENCE
I enjoy crosswords and word games I like to read I learn more from listening than from watching I like to tell jokes, stories, or tales I often listen to radio, TV, tapes, or CDs I enjoy writing; written words come easily and have meaning to me	I prefer team sports and being with people People come to me for advice I am empathetic I like to work out problems with a group I have a circle of friends and enjoy parties I am comfortable in a crowd; I am a leader I enjoy teaching others what I know
LOGICAL/MATHEMATICAL INTELLIGENCE	MUSICAL INTELLIGENCE
Math intrigues me I solve math problems easily I like using logic to solve problems I look for patterns, sequences, and organization I like setting up experiments and asking "what if" I use data in my work to measure, calculate, and analyze I can think in symbols and abstractions	I like to listen to musical selections I play a musical instrument or sing a lot I learn through music and rhythm I keep time to music and can follow a beat I often hum or sing as I walk or work I listen to music whenever possible I remember songs I sometimes create songs when I am learning something new
VISUAL/SPATIAL INTELLIGENCE	INTRAPERSONAL INTELLIGENCE
I think in pictures and organizational schemes I am sensitive to color, images, and design I use pictures, slides, and video to record data I draw and doodle, create charts Illustrations and graphic organizers help me learn I can find my way around unfamiliar areas I have a good sense of direction I can navigate using the sun or stars	I enjoy being alone to meditate, reflect, or think I like to learn more about myself I think about things and plan what to do next I have a realistic view of my abilities I am independent and confident I prefer to work alone I am aware of my strengths and weaknesses
BODILY/KINESTHETIC INTELLIGENCE	NATURALISTIC INTELLIGENCE
I enjoy movement and physical activity I like doing rather than watching I enjoy creating things with my hands I use my hands when speaking I learn through touch I like working with my hands on projects and hobbies I like to practice skills I am well coordinated	I enjoy spending time in nature Sounds of nature are fascinating or soothing I am happiest outdoors I know the names of plants, animals, rocks, and planets I know the names of natural things and like to classify them I like to investigate, explore, and discover I enjoy logical reasoning and probing questions

(Continued)

Figure 14 (Continued)

Type of Intelligence	Least Like Me			Most Like Me	
1. Verbal/Linguistic Intelligence	1	2	3	4	5
2. Logical/Mathematical Intelligence	1	2	3	4	5
3. Visual/Spatial Intelligence	1	2	3	4	5
4. Bodily/Kinesthetic Intelligence	1	2	3	4	5
5. Interpersonal Intelligence	1	2	3	4	5
6. Musical Intelligence	1	2	3	4	5
7. Intrapersonal Intelligence	1	2	3	4	5
8. Naturalistic Intelligence	1	2	3	4	5

SOURCE: Adapted from Gregory and Chapman, 2007.

PROPERTIES OF EARTH MATERIALS ALIGNED WITH MULTIPLE INTELLIGENCES: AN INSTRUCTIONAL APPROACH

Learning experiences and projects should be designed to enable students to use a variety of intelligences. Students will most likely select learning experiences that allow them to work primarily in areas of strength, but it is important to require them to work and develop skills in other areas as well. Providing a variety of pathways with choices allows students to spend more time developing concepts in meaningful ways rather than being forced to use a single approach based on a single intelligence.

Choice menu: Figure 15 is an example of a choice menu offering a variety of projects and activities for learning rocks and soil as part of a unit on properties of earth materials at the intermediate grade level. Teachers may wish to use some of the suggested activities as "anchor activities," those based on important concepts and designed for whole group instruction.

The choices for projects should include opportunities for relearning, reinforcing learning, and extending learning and be designed to address the goals and standards for the unit. Students may generate additional ideas for projects related to the instructional goals.

Unit goals and standards—students will learn the following:
- Earth materials are solid rocks, soil, water, and the gases of the atmosphere.

- Earth materials have different physical and chemical properties that make them useful in different ways.
- Soils have properties such as color, texture, ability to hold water, and ability to support plant growth.
- Fossils provide evidence about the plants and animals that lived long ago and provide information about the nature of past environments.

Additional Standards Addressed in Unit

Science and technology: understanding about science and technology, technological design, ability to distinguish between natural objects and objects made by humans.

Science in personal and social perspectives: types of earth resources and conservation.

Nature of science: science as a human endeavor.

A basic description is given for each activity on the choice board—more specific information and direction will be needed for students. Rock and mineral specimens, fossils, soil samples and testing kits, books, posters or newsprint and markers, computers with Internet access, and other materials and resources are required. Action plans, data, and written work can be recorded in notebooks.

Procedure: Following group instruction on anchor concepts, students are given a project menu from which they must select and complete four activities in one week—one activity from each box. In this example, the suggestions are divided into four categories based on a single intelligence or a combination of intelligences. Choice boards can be designed around other intelligences. The samples here are as follows:

1. Linguistic: activities that require reading, writing, and research.

2. Naturalistic and logical/mathematical: activities that require "doing": experiments, investigations, activities, and projects.

3. Bodily/kinesthetic, spatial, logical/mathematical: activities that require research, problem solving and reasoning, or technology.

4. Interpersonal: activities that require group participation, role playing, or action research.

Figure 15   Project Menu for Properties of Earth Materials

1. Linguistic: Reading and Writing	2. Naturalistic and Logical/Mathematical: Experiments, Projects, Investigations	3. Bodily/Kinesthetic, Logical/Mathematical, Spatial: Research, Problem Solving and Reasoning, or Technology Based	4. Interpersonal: Group Participation, Role-Playing, or Action Research
• Select a book or articles on minerals, soils, or fossils. Read about the topic and write a summary of your findings in your notebook. • Write an article for a newsletter explaining the rock cycle. • Select a book that provides information about rocks, soil, water, or gases in the atmosphere. Write a book report. • Research soil as a valuable resource. What are the greatest threats to this resource? What are some ways to conserve it?	• Identify and record the physical properties of each rock in a set (properties include color, luster, hardness, shape, and texture). Create a classification system based on observable properties. • Observe the properties of the mineral quartz. Compare it to the rock granite. How are they alike and different? • Follow directions for growing crystals. Make models of crystal shapes using card stock. Identify minerals that have each shape. • Collect rock samples and soil from an area. Use a tumbler to break down the rocks. Describe what happens. Observe the soil. Identify similarities and differences. • Compare the physical appearance of two or more types of soil. Record observations. Conduct tests on soil for texture, permeability, porosity, and ability to support plant growth. • Test soil samples for chemical properties using a soil testing kit. Make a chart to show findings. • Observe fossils in a set and record their properties. Align them on a Geologic Time Line. Identify similar organisms that exist today.	• Research and make a list of ways rocks and minerals are used in or around your home. Make drawings to show two ways rocks are used and two ways minerals are used. Display your work. • Interview classmates and make a list of questions they have about Earth's materials: rocks, soil, water, and gases in the atmosphere. Research answers to their questions. • Locate areas of the world on a map where precious metals like gold, silver, or platinum are found. Select one an conduct and in-depth study. Share your findings. • Research the economic importance of one or more gemstones (diamond, opal, sapphire, ruby, and so forth). • Visit a museum or store that has a display of rocks and minerals. Take pictures, if possible, and collect information about the materials. Share your findings.	• Prepare to give a short presentation on any one of the activities you did. Use visuals as part of the presentation. • Describe the most serious threats to soil. • Write a play to teach about something you learned about rocks, minerals, or fossils. Perform the play (with students or puppets) for a group of younger children. • Assemble a team of three paleontologists. Design a fossil hunting expedition. What fossils will you hunt? Where in the world will you go? What will you take? What will your "finds" tell you about life in the past and the nature of past environments? (If possible, interview a scientist to help plan your trip.) • Get involved in a park or community project to plant trees or shrubs. Learn about the types of soils required to support plant growth and the care of the plants.

STERNBERG'S VIEW OF INTELLIGENCE

Gardner's theory meshes well with Robert Sternberg's triarchic model (1996). Sternberg suggested that successful intelligence is the ability to use knowledge with creative intelligence, analytic intelligence, and practical intelligence. Knowledge in and of itself is nice to know, but to be truly valuable it must be used in an intelligent way.

Creative intelligence: This is the cognitive process we use to create questions, problems, and projects that validate new learning. This frequently involves challenging existing assumptions and removing obstacles in our quest for new ways to do things. It is really like "thinking outside the box."

Analytic intelligence: It is the type of thinking used to analyze new learning and to solve problems, make choices, and judge critically. It includes the ability to identify a problem, create strategies, offer solutions, muster resources and monitor their application, and evaluate results. Educational testing often focuses on this form of intelligence.

Practical intelligence: This is the pragmatic intelligence that draws on both the MI and the triarchic theories of intelligence. Practical intelligence enables students to learn, apply, and integrate academic knowledge about subject areas with knowledge about themselves (learning styles and intelligence profile), structure and learning of academic tasks, and the complex educational and social system. Action oriented, this intelligence puts learning to good use to solve problems and make decisions.

In classrooms, we can challenge students not only to know concepts, but to use and apply them in creative, analytical, and practical ways to deepen their understanding. The processes of using and applying knowledge engage a wide range of learners by enabling them to ask questions and make choices that relate to their learning styles and multiple intelligences.

LEARNING ACTIVITIES LINKED TO INTELLIGENCES

Figure 16 gives examples of the ways learning activities in the science classroom can address creative, analytical, and practical intelligence.

Figure 16   Learning Activities Linked to Sternberg's Intelligences

Creative	Analytical	Practical
• Make models, posters, or diagrams to explain a natural phenomenon • Find new or amusing ways to demonstrate a concept • Create new ways to use tools or equipment • Find a unique approach to solve a problem • Design investigations to answer inquiry questions • Improve on the design of a common product • Create conceptual models or a new invention • Make connections to other areas of the curriculum	• Describe the structure of an organism or natural object and describe its function • Demonstrate simple machines and explain how they make work easier • Make a diagram to show a complex system • Analyze a graph, chart, or diagram and explain its meaning • Create an analogy to explain cell structure and function • Write a step-by-step plan for solving a problem • Describe why a simple or complex machine works	• Identify ways science links to technology for practical purposes • Show ways to use ____ to solve a problem • Explain the importance of ____ to the economy • Design a plan for healthy meals and exercise • Develop a plan to use materials or resources for useful purposes • Investigate how a natural object is used in the home • Investigate how natural resources are used in the local community • Identify careers that are most closely associated with the natural sciences

INTELLIGENCES APPLIED TO A UNIT ON NUTRITION

Figure 17 shows a variety of ways that creative, analytical, and practical intelligences can be tapped through an intermediate or middle grade unit on nutrition.

Standard: Science in Personal and Social Perspectives—Personal Health

Figure 17   Intelligences Applied to a Unit on Nutrition

Creative	Analytical	Practical
Research and design a healthy menu for an ethnic restaurant of your choice. The menu items should be nutritionally sound as well as appealing.	Create a chart on which to record your meals for a week. Include breakfast, lunch, and supper as well as snacks.	Apply your understanding of nutrition by creating a healthy diet for yourself or for a friend who has a particular dietary need.

Creative	Analytical	Practical
Base your choices on your knowledge of nutrition. Be prepared to defend your choices.	Apply what you know about nutrition. Analyze the meals to determine their nutritional value.	Prepare to justify your plan.
Suggest ways to make patrons aware of the "healthy choices."	Evaluate your findings in relation to recommended daily allowances for your age and activity level. Make recommendations for change.	Design a poster to promote healthy eating habits.

STRATEGIES FOR PREASSESSMENT

The more teachers know about the different ways their students learn and interact with and process data, the better able they are to plan instruction that provides all students with opportunities for success.

Data about the ways students learn and process data can be obtained through the following:

- Observations of student behavior.
- Interviews and conversations.
- Notebook entries.
- Portfolios, projects, and products from previous grades.
- Survey instruments.
- Self assessments.

ASSESSING PRIOR KNOWLEDGE

What is it? Students come to the classroom with varying degrees of knowledge and understanding about concepts and principles and varying degrees of skills based on their formal and informal educational experiences as well as their personal experiences. Since new knowledge and skills are built on prior knowledge and skills, it is important that teachers have a good idea of what students know and are able to do prior to planning instruction.

Why do we do it? Using tools and strategies (such as the Inventory on page 44) to determine what students know and are able to do can uncover misconceptions students have about a topic and determine their levels of understanding and skills. Worthwhile learning activities and experiences are those that build on the students' knowledge base, further develop skills, and strengthen valued dispositions in some meaningful way.

SCIENCE INTEREST INVENTORY

Please help me get to know you better by completing the survey

Name: _____ Date: _____

1. My interest in science is: (circle one)   low   medium   high

2. The thing I love most about science is: _____

The thing I like least about science is: _____

3. My favorite area of science is: (circle one)

   Life Science   Earth/Space Science   Physical Science

4. My favorite way to learn science is through: (check all that apply)

☐ reading books and articles

☐ games and puzzles

☐ problem solving

☐ looking for patterns

☐ role playing

☐ experimenting

☐ collecting data about objects and events

☐ watching videos, slide shows, or PowerPoint presentations

☐ a variety of physical activities

☐ investigations outdoors or in the community

☐ exploring nature

☐ projects, such as making models

☐ caring for and studying animals

☐ working with others

☐ working alone

☐ using magnifiers and microscopes

☐ other: (please add) _____

The topic in science I would most like to learn about is: _____

Addressing Misconceptions

Researchers have identified hundreds of misconceptions that children and adults have about natural phenomena. Knowledge of common misconceptions for a topic enables teachers to watch for them in student responses, notebook entries, and discussions to guide students toward accurate concept understanding. If misconceptions are identified and addressed when important concepts are initially introduced, there is a greater chance of correcting them.

For example, a list of children's misconceptions about science was compiled by the Operation Physics Elementary/Middle School Physics Education Outreach Project of the American Institute of Physics. The author or editor is unknown (http://amasci.com/miscon/opphys.html).

Misconceptions that students have about the biosphere are as follows:

1. Coral reefs exist throughout the Gulf and North Atlantic waters.

2. Dinosaurs and cavemen lived at the same time.

3. Acquired characteristics can be inherited.

4. Winter weather can be predicted by studying the thickness of the fur of some animals.

5. Humans are responsible for the extinction of the dinosaurs.

6. Some human races have not evolved as much as others.

7. Evolution is goal-directed.

8. Evolutionary changes are driven by need.

The concepts underlying the misconceptions should be introduced at the primary and intermediate grades through inquiry-based investigations supported by information-based resources and built on in the middle grades. In this example, several misunderstandings relate to human evolution and inherited versus acquired traits. Instruction at the primary and intermediate grades dealing with heredity, geologic time, and other related topics is critical for providing a foundation for science courses at the middle and high school levels.

How do we do it? Preassessments may take the form of quizzes, tasks, surveys, conversations, or self-assessments. They are tools or strategies that enable teachers to learn the following:

- What students know about a unit topic.
- Student levels of concept understanding and skill ability.
- Misconceptions students have.
- Interest in the topic.

Pretest of Concepts

It is not unusual to give students a pretest of concepts that is the same as the posttest. Identifying misconceptions and finding out what students know prior to instruction help teachers adjust instruction to focus on student needs. Quizzes may take the form of forced response, open response, or performance tasks.

Pretests should address what students need to know and be able to do and include the following:

- Opportunities to explain and apply important concepts of the unit.
- Simple-to-complex and concrete-to-abstract understandings.
- Opportunities to create charts and graphs or data tables and analyze data.
- Opportunities to draw, create graphic organizers, or demonstrate understanding.

Pretest of Skills

Paper and pencil pretests can provide information related to students' knowledge of skills, but it is necessary to provide students with performance tasks to determine their levels of proficiency for manipulative skills. For example, at the primary level, skill levels might be assessed by giving students sets of natural objects and simple equipment and asking them to do the following:

a. Observe objects and describe their properties.
b. Sort the objects by properties and explain their groups.
c. Serial order objects by size.
d. Measure the objects by using formal or informal measurement tools.

At the intermediate or middle grade levels, students' skills can be assessed as they work through an investigation that requires them to make observations, classify, measure, and, in addition, do the following:

- Use tools and equipment.
- Identify variables.
- Collect and record data.
- Design data tables and create graphs.
- Draw conclusions.
- Make inferences based on observations or make predictions based on data.
- Apply concepts.
- Use logic and reasoning throughout.

Evidence of students' skill levels can be obtained through observation, notebook entries, data tables and graphs, discussion and discourse.

CONVERSATION CARDS FOR PREASSESSMENT

Conversation cards enable students to become aware of new terms and concepts prior to instruction. Through this activity, teachers can gain insight about what students know and the misconceptions and questions students have. Through the activity and discussion, students can assess their prior knowledge and understanding and learn from other students. The information gained from the activity will help teachers determine the direction for instruction.

Prior to instruction, students are given a set of cards with important vocabulary words and concepts that relate to the unit. Include some blank cards in the set. Cards may range in number and complexity based on the grade level or ability levels of students. Students should work in groups of two or three to allow for interaction and sharing of ideas.

Students should be directed to sort or classify the cards in any way that makes sense or is meaningful to them. They should set aside any cards with words or concepts that are unfamiliar.

Students should record the terms and concepts that they know and don't know in their notebooks and describe or draw the system they used to sort the cards. They should identify questions they have about the topic. Engage students in a discussion through which they can share the ways they sorted the cards, their understandings and misconceptions, and their questions.

Following instruction, students may be given the set of cards again and asked to sort or classify them with new group members. Here they may add new ideas or concepts they learned and integrate them into the categories they created. The activity enables students to assess themselves through a discussion of what they know. In addition, they can reinforce learning, identify what they do not know, and ask and record new questions.

A set of conversation cards for an intermediate or middle grade unit on population and ecosystems might include the following:

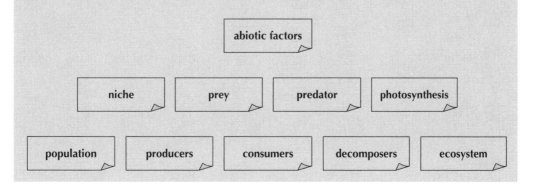

PART II

Designing Differentiated Instruction

The chapters in Part II further explain the variety of methods, effective practices, and strategies for differentiating instruction that are found in the Planning Model in Figure 3. The instructional design phases of the model are based on the 5E's Lesson Plan Format (Engage, Explore, Explain, Extend, and Evaluate) that has become popular in science education. The chapters that follow introduce methods and strategies for effective teaching and learning and describe strategies that can be useful for differentiating instruction at each of the five phases.

4 Methods and Effective Practices for Increasing Student Achievement

O nce the classroom climate for effective instruction is created, the goals and standards for science for each grade level are identified and understood, and information is known about student learning styles, personal intelligences, and cultural perspectives, teachers can design instruction to meet the needs and interests of their students. Instruction is a creative process involving an array of multisensory activities and experiences that challenge the mind, stir the emotions, provide social interaction and physical challenges, and satisfy the human needs to learn and to know oneself. Instruction should mirror life and offer learners a wide range of opportunities to construct an understanding of the natural world. Prior knowledge of what students know and are able to do will provide a starting point from which teachers can build concept understanding and develop skills by utilizing methods and practices that are most appropriate for their students.

METHODS FOR TEACHING AND LEARNING SCIENCE

What are they? Methods are the various ways we can approach learning in the classroom. They are the choices that are made by teachers (or by students) about how students will learn. The methods that are selected and used by teachers are linked to their belief systems and self-efficacy as well as to the expectations of administrators, parents, and students. High quality instruction includes the use of a variety of methods. Instruction in science is a function of the interaction of five basic methods:

- **Expository**—lectures, media presentations, guest speakers, text material, pictures, CDs, audio and video tapes, trade books, and such.
- **Discussion**—student to student or teacher to student exchange of ideas and information.
- **Demonstration**—presentation by teachers, students, or invited guests with or without interactions and discussion.
- **Guided inquiry**—student- or teacher-generated questions and activities with varying degrees of structure leading to a range of predictable or fairly predictable outcomes or expectations.
- **Open inquiry or problem-based learning**—student- or teacher-generated inquiry questions or ill-structured problems without predicted outcomes or expectations.

Why do we use them? Methods are the means to the end, that is, they are the ways that instruction is designed to successfully address and meet goals and objectives for learning. Varying methods throughout instruction provide the greatest opportunity to capture and maintain student interest, motivate students, and maximize learning.

What do they look like?

Expository learning: Expository learning takes the form of receiving facts or information; reading stories, articles or text material; copying information; viewing a film or videotape; or listening to a lecture.

Discussion: Discussion engages students in dialog related to facts, findings, or opinions. Environments that encourage discussion are non-threatening and respectful of students' thoughts and ideas and understandings or misunderstandings. Discussions are especially useful following investigations or research for reflecting on processes, sharing and analyzing data, determining validity of conclusions, applying concepts, and creating meaning.

Demonstration: Demonstrations involve one or more persons giving a presentation to an audience that may vary in size from a small group to an entire class. Demonstrations may be valuable or necessary when

- The materials or equipment involved is costly or delicate.
- The equipment, materials, or process is not safe for students to use themselves.
- A visitor is showing or describing work or a small set of samples that are fragile or valuable.
- There is a person or animal involved.
- Safety is an issue.
- There is only one opportunity for an event to happen.

Demonstrations with interactions allow students to have input and to ask questions.

Guided inquiry: Inquiry is an active learning process that begins with one or more questions developed by the teacher or generated by students. The heart of inquiry is investigation, and investigations are rooted in "hands-on" or "minds-on" activities and experiences. Through the process of inquiry, data are generated that either support or do not support predictions or hypotheses. As students engage in discussion and reflection, they realize the role and importance of data for supporting their conclusions.

Inquiry investigations are, by nature, interdisciplinary. Science naturally integrates with mathematics, literacy, technology, social studies, the arts, and other areas of the curriculum. For example:

- Graphs can be used to display data sets.
- Reading can be enhanced through trade books and reference books that define concepts, provide information, and explain relationships between concepts.
- Notebooks can be used to record information, inquiry questions, background information, action plans, data, and explanations and summaries of learning, while providing opportunities for students to use vocabulary in meaningful ways.
- Technology and software programs offer novel approaches for learning, practice, relearning important concepts, and applying and extending learning.

Open inquiry and problem-based learning: In open inquiry, students generate questions and design action plans to access and use information, investigate and collect data, and draw conclusions based on their findings.

Inquiry questions may be generated prior to instruction as things they want to know or during instruction as new questions arise while learning occurs.

Sample Inquiry Questions

- Do marigolds that are kept in the light 24 hours per day grow taller than those that are kept in the light 8 hours a day?
- Which frozen liquid melts the fastest: water, milk, or soda? Which liquid evaporates the fastest?
- Does your pulse rate increase or decrease after listening to music?
- Do plants grow better if they are grown with music? Would the kind of music affect the results?
- Do batteries stored in the freezer power a toy car longer than those stored at room temperature?
- Do pumpkins that weigh five pounds or more contain more seeds than those that weigh less than five pounds?
- Does the size of the wheels on a toy car affect the distance it travels down a ramp?
- Does the temperature of water affect how fast salt crystals (or sugar crystals) dissolve or disappear?
- Do model airplanes with large wings fly farther than those with smaller wings?

Summary: All of the methods have a place in inquiry-based science. It is important that students understand that scientists use a variety of methods and strategies for discovering natural phenomena and constructing knowledge.

Expository methods are useful for providing interesting and relevant information, generating interest, and reinforcing or relearning concepts.

Demonstrations provide visual displays of phenomena that are often exciting for the observer. They may take the form of discrepant events that activate brain cells by causing cognitive conflict. Such conflict generates new inquiry questions.

Discussion that includes reflection on process and the sharing of ideas, data, conclusions, applications, and meaning is an important part of every investigation.

The process of inquiry focuses on questions that are of interest to students and capitalizes on the sense of wonder that motivates students to learn. A learning cycle approach begins with questions based on major concepts, issues, or problems. Students assume the role of "scientist" as they explore and investigate natural phenomena, collect and process data, formulate conclusions, create meaning, make connections and apply learning, and generate new questions.

In problem-based learning, "ill-structured" problems are posed by teachers or students and students are challenged to investigate and offer varied solutions based on their research. Problems may be designed to lead students toward content-rich investigations that have relevant applications leading to a deep understanding of issues, but not predetermined outcomes. Often alternative solutions are offered and considered.

The Roles of Teachers and Students in Methods

Figure 18 identifies the roles of teachers and students in the various methods. Note the methods that engage students in active versus passive ways of learning.

RESEARCH-BASED EFFECTIVE PRACTICES

What are they? Effective practices are instructional strategies that have been shown to increase student motivation, interest, and achievement. They are "brain-based" in that they capitalize on the brain's natural abilities and promote student learning. Effective science classrooms engage students in inquiry-based investigations, focus on developing understanding of important concepts and principles, develop student responsibility for learning, incorporate formative assessment, and encourage cooperative and collaborative approaches to learning.

Why do we use them? Research is critical to the practitioner in that it identifies practices that enhance student achievement and provide a strong rationale for the application of the practices to classroom instruction. Recently researchers have concluded that the most important factor affecting student learning is the teacher (Sanders & Horn, 1994, and Wright, Horn, & Sanders, 1997, in Marzano, Pickering, & Pollack, 2001; Wenglinsky, 2000). Research-based effective practices offer important messages to teachers about what works, providing valuable insights and information to guide them in planning instruction, monitoring and directing learning, and assessing the effectiveness of the instructional process.

Figure 18 Roles of Teachers and Students in Methods

Methods	What Teachers Will Do	What Students Will Do
Expository	• Lecture, provide information • Invite a speaker • Read or tell a story • Provide books, pictures, audio and video tapes, films, software, and other sources of information	• Read about a topic • Watch videotapes or presentations • Listen to a tape or music • Listen to a lecture or talk • Access and use information
Demonstration	• Conduct an experiment or activity, show a discrepant event, or explain a process or product while students observe • Engage in discussion with students during the demonstration (optional)	• Observe a product, process, or event • Observe and discuss a discrepant event
Discussion	• Ask questions • Interact verbally with students • Guide student-student verbal interaction	• Engage in conversation with the teacher or students • Listen • Ask and answer questions
Guided Inquiry	• Structure learning environment to meet needs of students • Engage students by creating a meaningful context and offering options • Ask or elicit inquiry questions • Design and facilitate activities and experiences • Check for misconceptions • Check accuracy of work • Guide instruction through questions and cues • Mediate and support • Challenge students to think and create meaning • Assess to monitor learning and guide instruction	• Participate in an activity or experience to answer one or more teacher or student-generated questions • Choose learning pathways and grouping patterns • Design action plans for investigating inquiry questions • Investigate and manipulate equipment and materials • Keep a notebook • Communicate, reflect, apply learning, create meaning • Apply and extend learning • Engage in research
Open Inquiry	• Encourage students to think, inquire, plan, research, and be involved in learning • Mediate and guide, as needed, to assure purposeful pursuits • Be flexible and supportive • Provide equipment, materials, resources, advice, and encouragement, as needed	• Ask questions, design action plans, engage in activities and experiences, share findings, and apply and extend learning • Confer with teachers, as needed • Investigate problems or issues • Keep a notebook • Take or share responsibility for learning • Share results and data • Consider alternative solutions • Ask new questions

What do they look like? The NSES identify effective practices for teaching science. Recommendations for teachers include the following:

1. Understanding and responding to student needs, interests, and strengths.

2. Learning science through investigation and inquiry.

3. Understanding concepts and developing abilities of inquiry.

4. Learning subject matter in the context of inquiry, science in personal and social perspective, technology, and history and nature of science.

5. Using activities that investigate and analyze science questions.

6. Designing investigations that focus on content and use process skills in context

7. Using evidence and strategies to develop or revise explanations.

8. Assessing what is most highly valued.

9. Continuously assessing student understanding and sharing responsibility for learning with students. (National Research Council, 1996, pp. 52, 72, 100, and 113)

A meta-analysis of research on instruction conducted at the Mid-continent Research for Education and Learning (McREL) identified nine strategies that have a high probability of enhancing student achievement for all students (Marzano, Pickering, & Pollack, 2001). The effective practices are as follows:

1. Identifying similarities and differences.

2. Summarizing and note taking.

3. Reinforcing effort and providing recognition.

4. Assigning homework and practice time.

5. Creating nonlinguistic representations.

6. Cooperative learning.

7. Setting objectives and providing feedback.

8. Generating and testing hypotheses.

9. Activating prior knowledge through questions, cues, and advance organizers.

The authors of the study made it clear that all strategies may not be effective for all students in all subject areas. They recommended that teachers rely on their knowledge of their students, their subject matter, and their situations to identify the strategies that are most appropriate for them.

STRATEGIES LINKED TO BRAIN RESEARCH AND CLASSROOM PRACTICES

The practices are rooted in brain-based learning and active inquiry. Figure 19 shows some ways that research can be used to inform brain-based instruction. The left column identifies the nine Marzano research-based instructional strategies by decreasing percentile rank. The center column describes findings from brain research that support the strategies as effective practices for learning. The right-hand column identifies characteristics of inquiry-based science that relate to the practices.

Gordon Cawalti (1995) edited a handbook of research on student achievement and identified effective practices for improving science instruction. These findings, compiled by Dorothy Gabel, include the following:

1. Using a learning cycle approach.

2. Using computers to collect and display data.

3. Using analogies, which enable the learner to compare the familiar to the unfamiliar

4. Using wait time and computer simulations.

5. Using student-generated and teacher-generated concept maps.

6. Using cooperative learning for classroom and laboratory instruction.

7. Using systematic approaches to problem solving and real-life situations.

8. Using a science-technology-society approach.

9. Using discrepant events for cognitive conflict and enhanced concept understanding.

Science Notebooks As Tools for Learning

Using notebooks in science has been shown to increase student achievement in science and other areas of the curriculum (Klentschy, Garrison, & Maia Amaral, 2000).

Figure 19   Effective Strategies, Brain Research, and Classroom Applications

Effective Strategies	Brain Research	Classroom Applications
Identifying Similarities and Differences	The brain seeks patterns, connections, and relationships between and among prior and new learning	• Classify objects and phenomena • Compare and contrast • Use Venn diagrams to compare characteristics of organisms or events • Write analogies for important concepts • Trace the history of inventions, theories, or technology; compare past with present • Describe relationships between prior knowledge (or misconceptions) and new learning • Create metaphors
Summarizing and Note Taking	The brain pays attention to meaningful information and deletes that which is not relevant	• Use notebooks to record information and summarize learning • Use jigsaw to emphasize important concepts • Differentiate between relevant and irrelevant data
Reinforcing Effort and Providing Recognition	The brain responds to challenge and not threat. Emotions enhance learning	• Provide a safe, comfortable, student-centered environment • Provide activities that are relevant, interesting and challenging • Provide continuous support and recognition
Assigning Homework and Practice	"If you don't use it, you lose it." Practice and rehearsal make learning "stick"	• Apply concepts and principles to student lives, technology, and society • Use games and puzzles to reinforce concepts • Reinforce learning through reading and extensions
Generating Nonlinguistic Representations	The brain is a parallel processor. Visual stimuli is recalled with 90% accuracy	• Create mind maps and graphic organizers, data tables and graphs • Draw pictures and illustrations to record observations of organisms and events and change over time • Create two- and three-dimensional models
Using Cooperative Learning	The brain is social. Collaboration facilitates understanding and higher order thinking	• Use lab partners and flexible grouping patterns • Create jigsaw experiences • Use and vary cooperative and collaborative strategies
Setting Objectives and Providing Feedback	The brain responds to high challenge and continues to strive with continuous feedback	• Communicate clear targets and learning goals • Use formative assessment strategies to monitor student learning • Provide continuous feedback • Use rubrics to guide instruction and for self-assessment • Maintain high standards and expectations
Generating and Testing Hypotheses	The brain is curious and has an innate need to make meaning through patterns	• Design standards-related inquiries based on student- or teacher-generated questions • Generate a hypotheses and create action plans for testing • Use questions to reflect on process and data and create meaning • Apply learning to personal lives and events within the local and global communities

SOURCE: Modified from Gregory and Parry, 2006

Notebook pages can be designed by the teacher or by students to record details of activities and experiences. Students can record their inquiry questions and observations; write action plans; draw pictures, illustrations, and graphic organizers; create data tables and graphs; explain understanding; and summarize learning and extended learning. The notebook is also a tool for formative assessment as it provides evidence of student work and learning throughout a unit.

A science notebook might include any or all of these components:

- Inquiry questions or problems of interest
  - Student- or teacher-generated.
  - Worthy of investigation.
- Prediction or hypothesis
  - Relates to inquiry question.
  - Relies on prior knowledge or experience.
- Action plan for investigating inquiry question
  - Relates to inquiry question.
  - Identifies equipment and materials needed.
  - Clearly identifies reasonable, sequenced steps.
  - Identifies variables, when appropriate.
- Observations and data
  - Qualitative and quantitative observations.
  - Data are relevant and shown on a table or chart.
- Graphics and graphs
  - Visual(s) to show process, change, or data and relationships between concepts.
  - Show relationships between variables in an experiment.
- Reflections and conclusions
  - Analysis of process and findings.
  - Insights or answers related to inquiry question.
  - Use of evidence to support conclusions.
- Applications and creating meaning
  - Link to prior knowledge and personal life.
  - Connections to technology and society.
- Summaries of learning
  - Frame thought.
  - Describe learning.
- New questions and next steps

Lab Reports

Lab reports may follow a standard framework or be designed to relate more specifically to certain laboratory activities. Lab reports may be separate from or part of a notebook, depending on the teacher's preference.

Lab reports reflect an understanding of content through the ability to design, conduct, and communicate the results of an experiment. In addition, the report communicates the purpose, background understanding, procedures, findings, and conclusions.

The components of a lab report are as follows:

- Title of the lab.
- The purpose, including the inquiry question, objective of the investigation, and the dependent and independent variables, if applicable.
- Background information or a survey of literature.
- Procedures: a step-by-step process that describes what will be done and how it will be done.
- Data and calculations: data should be shown on labeled data tables.
- Graphs of data: graphs should be appropriately labeled and clear.
- Discussion of results and the conclusions that can be drawn from the data; conclusions should be supported with logic and data; discuss the implications and meaning of the findings of the study.
- Suggestions for additional needed research if data are not conclusive.
- Applications to technology and society.
- New questions.
- Bibliography (if applicable).

Figure 20 shows an outline for a lab report.

Scoring Rubric for a Lab Report

Some components of the report may take several pages, such as background information, data tables and graphs, and applications. The framework will help to guide the students, especially if a rubric is provided. Figure 21 shows a sample scoring rubric for a lab report.

Grouping

What is it? Basically, there are four grouping patterns: whole group, small groups, partners, and individuals. There are times when instruction is suitable for large groups and times when activities are most effective when students work in smaller groups or with partners.

Figure 20   Lab Report

Name: _____   Date: _____

Title of Lab: _____

Description of Lab:

Inquiry Question:

Objective(s):

Background Information or Literature Review:

Procedures:

Data Tables, Graphs, and Calculations:

Conclusions and Additional Research:

Applications to Technology and Society:

New Questions:

Bibliography:

Figure 21 Scoring Rubric for a Lab Report

Part of Report	Exceeds Expectations (3)	Meets Expectations (2)	Does Not Meet Expectations (1)	Is Not Present
Title	Title is creative or unique	Title is shown and appropriate	Title does not fit investigation	Title is missing
Description	Identifies key concepts; is clear, detailed and accurate; identifies inquiry question and objective(s); identifies and explains variables	Identifies key concepts; is clear and accurate; identifies inquiry question, objective(s), and variables	Description is not accurate or is lacking detail related to inquiry question, objectives, or variables	Description is missing or inquiry question, objectives, or variables are not described or are missing
Background Information	Includes detailed information from two or more reputable sources of various types	Includes information from two reputable sources	Information is minimal or from a single source	Information is lacking or from an unreliable source
Procedures	Describes a detailed and accurate approach for safely gathering relevant data and addressing the inquiry question	Describes an accurate approach to gathering relevant data to address inquiry question	Description is lacking in detail or inappropriate; approach does not address inquiry question	Procedures missing
Data Tables, Graphs, Calculations	Tables and graphs are well-designed, accurate, and labeled; all calculations are shown and explained	Tables and graphs are accurate and labeled; calculations are shown	Tables and graphs are incomplete or inaccurate or labels or calculations are lacking	Tables, graphs, or calculations are missing
Conclusions and Research Needs	Conclusions are logical, data based, and explained; research needs are identified, if appropriate, and explained	Conclusions are logical and based on data; research needs are identified, if appropriate	Conclusions are not based on data; additional research needs are lacking or inappropriate	Conclusions or additional research needs, if relevant, are missing
Applications to Technology and Society	Concepts are applied to technology or society with detailed explanations and examples or resources	Concept(s) are applied to technology or society with examples and resources cited	Concept application is weak or minimal	Concept application is lacking
New Questions	Questions show insight or ingenuity	Questions relate to inquiry and are relevant to content	Questions do not relate to content being studied	Questions are missing
Bibliography	Exceeds required number and variety of relevant resources in appropriate format	Includes the required number and variety of relevant resources	Resources lacking in number, variety, or relevance	Resources are not cited

Instruction designed for a whole group may include brainstorming and decision making, demonstrations, guest speakers, video presentations, and anchor activities that include discussion for reflection and meaning making. Small groups and partners work well for lab activities and outdoor investigations, projects, stations, enrichment or relearning activities, tutoring, and peer review. Some students may prefer to work alone on projects, investigations, or research.

Why do we use it? Students are grouped to meet their instructional, emotional, and personal needs. Some students learn best while working alone while others work better in small groups or with partners. Grouping students by prior knowledge and skill levels (readiness levels), learning preferences, and interests offers multiple opportunities for success.

In a group, each student brings talents such as verbal fluency, creativity, empathy, or technical expertise, and students are provided an opportunity to share their talents. Goleman (1995) found that the most important factor in maximizing the excellence of a group's product was the degree to which the members were able to create a state of internal harmony. Altering grouping patterns throughout the instructional process maximizes the opportunities for meeting social needs and for this harmony to occur.

What does it look like? Because grouping is based on a number of different variables and is a dynamic process, there is no single way to do it. Flexible grouping is the best approach to capitalizing on each student's strengths and enhancing learning.

Some of the factors on which grouping can be based are as follows:

- Knowledge of content or readiness for learning based on preassessments or test data.
- Nature of the instruction.
- Types and amount of equipment and consumable materials.
- Availability of resources such as books, models, computers, tutors or aides, and the like.
- Learning profiles.
- Interest.

Cooperative Learning

When we put students in groups, there are many things that can go wrong. Students take over, don't work on task, talk about other things, become social loafers, or wind up dysfunctional and unable to resolve conflict. If we use the guidelines for cooperative group learning, students in groups usually work better together and actually accomplish the academic task and develop social skills.

What is it? Cooperative group learning is an instructional strategy where students work collaboratively to accomplish an academic task while also practicing a social skill.

Why do we do it? We know that the brain is social and needs to discuss and share ideas and perspectives. Discussion clarifies thoughts and checks for understanding. It is a great assessment tool as teachers 'eavesdrop' on groups and notice misconceptions that need to be clarified.

In a differentiated classroom, students will move in and out of a variety of partner and group situations and, therefore, need to know how to work well together. Cooperative group learning has a proven track record based on sound research that shows actual gains in student achievement (Johnson & Johnson, 1981, cited in Bellanca & Fogarty, 1991; Lou et al., 1996; Marzano et al., 2001).

What does it look like? Science instruction lends itself well to cooperative learning since many investigations and experiences are best accomplished in small groups or with partners. There are five elements (Johnson & Johnson, 1981, cited in Gregory & Parry, 2006) that need to be a part of cooperative learning experiences:

- **Positive interdependence:** Making sure that students need one another by giving them a common goal, shared resources, tasks or roles, a suitable environment, an outside force (i.e., time limits).
- **Individual accountability**: Every student must be accountable for the knowledge or skill practiced in the group (e.g., presentation, report, quiz).
- **Face-to-face interaction:** An environment conducive for learning.
- **Collaborative or social skills:** Practice one or more social skills that students need.
- **Group processing:** Discussing how well they did with the social skill.

Teachers should structure group activities and individual student roles around these elements in ways that enable all students to be successful.

Adjustable Assignments

What are they? In classrooms everywhere, we are examining how we can get a better fit for all students. Adjustable assignments allow teachers to help students focus on essential skills and understanding key concepts, recognizing that they may be at different levels of readiness. Some may or may not be able to handle different levels of complexity or abstraction. Although the assignment is adjusted for different groups of learners, the standards, concepts, or content of each assignment have the same focus and each student has the opportunity to develop essential skills and understanding at his or her appropriate level of challenge. The activities better ensure that students explore ideas at their level while building on prior knowledge and experiencing incremental growth.

Why do we use them? Using adjusted assignments allows students to begin learning where they are and to work on challenging and worthwhile tasks. If we were growing flowers and some of the seeds had sprouted and were ready to flower, we would not pull them out by the roots and make them start again from seed. It sounds a bit bizarre when we think about it. We of course would give the plants that were advanced in their growth the light, water, and food they need and would nurture the seedlings that were just sprouting to help them bloom and grow.

Adjusting assignments allows for reinforcement or extension of concepts based on student readiness, learning styles, or multiple intelligence preferences. Appropriate adjustments in the learning have a greater chance of providing a "flow" experience in which each student is presented with challenging work that just exceeds his or her skill level.

The chances of success for each learner are increased because success is within reach, and ultimately reaching success will be highly motivating. Adjusting assignments also decreases the chances of "downshifting" and the sense of helplessness that students feel when a challenge is beyond their capabilities.

How do we use them? Initially, as in any planning process, the concepts, skills, and content that will be the focus of the activity are identified and aligned with targeted standards and expectations.

Using some method of preassessment (e.g., quizzes, journal entries, class discussions and data collection techniques, learning profiles, etc.), teachers gather data to determine the prior knowledge of students for the new content or the skill that is targeted for learning. The preassessment data are compiled. Then the key standards and concepts to be taught during the unit are determined. The teacher then decides which parts of the study should be taught to the total class and how they will be presented. The appropriate places to teach these concepts or skills are determined. Then comes the time to make decisions about any adjustable assignment. Assignments are adjusted to meet the needs of learners based on their present knowledge or skill level. The following are questions the teacher will answer when making decisions about these assignments.

- What content does each of the groups already know?
- What does each group need to learn?
- What strategies should be used to facilitate the learning of each portion?
- What is the most effective way to group for each activity?
- What assessment tools will be used so that students will be accountable?
- Are the plans meeting the individual needs of the students?

What do they look like? Basic knowledge and experience vary among learners, so adjustable assignments may be needed. Here is an example that is typical of what teachers face every time they start planning for all of their students.

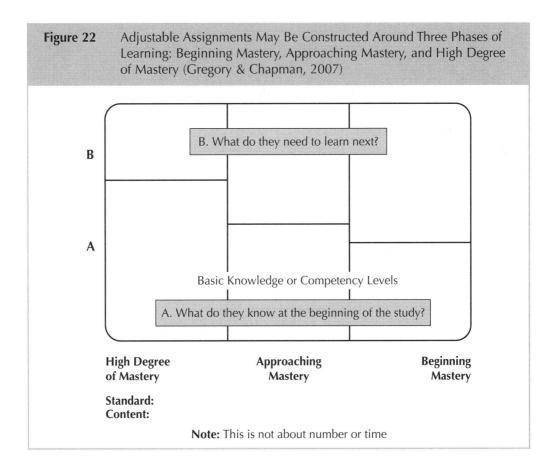

Figure 22 Adjustable Assignments May Be Constructed Around Three Phases of Learning: Beginning Mastery, Approaching Mastery, and High Degree of Mastery (Gregory & Chapman, 2007)

ADJUSTABLE ASSIGNMENTS FOR FORCE AND MOTION AT THE MIDDLE GRADE LEVEL

A unit of instruction dealing with force and motion at the middle grade level will require students to have a working knowledge and comprehension of basic terms such as force, motion, inertia, mass, acceleration, direction, magnitude, speed, and unbalanced forces. Students at a beginning mastery level may work in partners or small groups to operationally define these terms through hands-on activities or demonstrations at stations or centers. Other options for introducing important terminology include reading reference books, watching a videotape, or visiting a science center.

Students approaching mastery are ready to apply the terms to activities and investigations that relate directly to the key concepts found in state science standards. Such concepts are likely to be similar to those found in the NSES:

- The motion of an object can be described by its position, direction of movement, and speed.
- An object that is not being subjected to a force will continue to move at a constant speed and in a straight line.
- If more than one force acts on an object along a straight line, the forces will reinforce or cancel one another, depending on their direction and magnitude. Unbalanced forces will cause changes in the speed or direction of an object's motion (National Research Council, 1996).

As students test hypotheses and answer questions related to linear and nonlinear motion, they will learn about contributions of scientists like Aristotle, who attempted to clarify motion; Copernicus, who formulated a theory that the earth moved around the sun; Galileo, who supported the Copernican theory of the solar system through observation and experimentation; and Newton, who developed the famous three laws of motion.

Students with a high degree of mastery may already be familiar with the key concepts and are ready to apply these to more complex situations. For example, they may study force and motion in the context of amusement park rides, aerodynamics, or space exploration. They may study how the principles of force and motion apply to community problems or issues or to other areas of science, such as the dynamic forces in nature experienced through volcanic eruption, earthquakes, and mountain building, or forces that affect living things such as phototropism, geotropism, and gravity.

Curriculum Compacting

What is it? Curriculum compacting is a strategy first shared by Joe Renzulli of the University of Connecticut (Reis & Renzulli, 1992; see also Tomlinson, 1999, 2001). It provides for the student who is very capable and knowledgeable in a particular topic in a subject area. It is a way of maximizing time for the more advanced learner.

Why do we use it? Many students, because of prior experience, interests, and opportunities, may bring to the topic prior knowledge and skills that have been acquired over time. These may have been acquired through voracious reading, travel, and personal interest about a topic or from a mentor or role model who has had an influence on the learner. It is for these students that compacting may be used on occasion to enrich their curriculum, enhance and stretch their thinking, and help them develop into more self-directed learners. In many classrooms, where teaching to the middle is the norm, some learners are bored as they "repeat history," and others are lost because they don't have the background or experience they need to understand or be able to do what is expected of them.

Compacting or enriching may be used with the high-end or advanced learner(s) identified after a preassessment is given. It is important to allow all learners to move at their own pace, thus creating the "relaxed alertness" that Caine and Caine (1997) suggested. Challenging experiences that are perceived as "doable" in a learning situation put students into a state of "flow," thus engaging them at their level of challenge and not frustrating or boring them by giving them too difficult or too easy a task.

How do we do it? There are three phases that must be considered when using this approach:

Phase 1. In this phase, after an exploratory session where students are able to access prior knowledge and discuss their initial concepts and knowledge, a preassessment is given. This may be in the form of the following:

- A pretest.
- A conference where the learner shares knowledge and understanding about the topic.
- A portfolio presentation in which students show evidence of their comprehension and skill level (any or all of these may be used).

Phase 2. After the preassessment, the teacher analyzes the data and identifies what the student already knows and has mastered and what the student still needs to learn.

This additional knowledge or skill may be acquired by the following:

- Joining the total class group for that concept or information.
- Independent study.
- Homework assignments.
- Collaborating with a mentor or learning buddy in or outside school.
- Online learning.

Figure 23   Curriculum Compacting to Enrich Learning

Phase 1	Phase 2 Analyze data	Phase 3
Exploratory Phase	**Mastery:** skills, concepts What have they mastered?	**Advanced Level Challenges**
Preassessment: • Test • Confidence • Portfolio conference	**Needs to Master:** What do they need to know?	• Investigation • Problem-Based Learning • Service Learning • Project • Contract
To Find Out What the Learner • Knows • Needs to know • Wants to know	**How Will They Learn It?** • Gain with whole class • Independent study • Homework • Menter/buddy in or out of school • Online learning	**Opportunities for Successful Intelligence (Sternberg, 1996)** • Analytical • Practical • Creative **Assessment**

Phase 3. Once the missing pieces have been added, the students may choose or be offered the following:

- An investigation or research project.
- An ill-structured problem to solve.
- A service learning opportunity.
- A project.
- A negotiated contract.
- A special assignment.

These assignments facilitate the challenge of applying their knowledge and skill in a practical and creative way. As we noted in Chapter 3, Robert Sternberg (1996) defined "successful intelligence" as including the aspects of being analytical, practical, and creative, not just knowing.

Implementing compacting: This approach not only allows learners to enhance their understanding but also enables them to obtain an added perspective on the subject matter. Used with academically gifted or talented students, compacting may be done as a pullout or partial pullout model or orchestrated in the classroom with the subject teacher. If students are pulled out, they should not miss other subject areas of study that they have not mastered. Teachers must be sure that students really do have full mastery of the concept, not just surface-level knowledge. Students should not be required to complete the regular classroom assignments in the subject for which they have compacted out.

5 Strategies for Activating and Engaging

STRATEGIES FOR ENGAGEMENT

What are they? Strategies that activate and engage are creative ways to capture student attention and focus attention on a topic or concept.

Why do we use them? They are useful in every step of the instructional process to activate students mentally and physically. Strategies for stimulating interest include the following: K-W-L (Know-Want to Know-Learned) charts; demonstrations and discrepant events; stories and case studies related to community, state, national, or global problems or issues; school site investigations; field experiences; and guest presenters. Engagement is also a good time to identify student misconceptions about a topic so that these can be addressed, and hopefully reversed, through instruction.

What do they look like? Graphic organizers may be used to introduce essential questions or key concepts. Several different types of organizers may be presented with sets of key concepts from a unit of study. Students may be challenged to create a graphic to show relationships between concepts and, as the unit progresses, they may begin to identify specific relationships. By the time they have completed the unit, they should be able to show and explain relationships between concepts on a graphic organizer. The natural world is alive with amazing organisms and phenomena that are of interest to children. Creative strategies can be used to create wonder, generate questions and interest, and motivate students to learn about a topic. Underlying the use of strategies is the belief that brain-based strategies provide opportunities for students to learn in unique and exciting ways.

K-W-L Charts

Teachers are familiar with K-W-L charts that are often used to record student prior knowledge of a topic or concept. Asking students what they know about a topic or concept prompts them to describe prior knowledge or misconceptions. Brainstorming ideas or asking students to think about what they want to learn and how they want to learn also engages students in thinking. When students are able to act on their own questions, ideas, or suggestions, they take ownership for their learning.

Student responses provide a starting point for instruction whether that is building on concepts or addressing misconceptions. The K-W-L chart provides a visual for recording what students know, questions that students have about the topic or concept, and what was learned. Students can compare what they wanted to learn with what they learned and identify what they still want to learn about a topic. Figure 24 shows a K-W-L chart.

Figure 24   K-W-L Chart

What We Know	What We Want to Know	What We Learned

Discrepant Events

Discrepant events arouse interest and curiosity. Because these events are counterintuitive, that is, they show something that is counter to what one thinks is likely to happen, they cause cognitive conflict, which promotes questions, investigations, and discussions that, ultimately, enhance concept understanding.

The events should be based on standards-based concepts or principles and presented in ways that do not reveal the underlying principles. The events will have a mysterious quality. It is important for students to learn the "science" behind these events. They should be encouraged to ask questions based on their observations and suggest ways to answer them through activities and experiences that develop the concept or principle.

Discrepant Events for K–4 Science

- **Properties of air**
  Concept: Air is all around us; it occupies space, has weight, exerts pressure, and expands when heated. Air contains oxygen.

  Activity 1

  Use plastic bags to "catch air"; discuss what is filling the bag

  Push a wad of paper to the bottom of a plastic cup. Invert the cup and force it to the bottom of a container of water. Take the cup out and observe the paper. Discuss why is the paper is dry.

  Does air take up space? Refer to the "air catcher" and inflated balloons and basketballs. Discuss how air prevented the paper from becoming wet.

  Activity 2

  Use a shoe box with a hole in the side to snuff out a burning candle.

  Line up the hole about five cm from the burning candle and tap on the top of the box. Discuss what caused the candle to burn out.

  What do you use to blow out birthday candles? Does the air we take into our lungs take up space? How do you know? Does moving air create a force? Give examples.

- **Properties of earth materials**
  Concept: Water changes from liquid to gas through the process of evaporation.

  Activity 1

  Place two containers with equal amounts of water on the window sill.

  Place a cover over one container. Observe the water levels in the two containers throughout a week. Discuss what happens to water when left in an open container.

  Activity 2

  Observe puddles after a rain. Discuss what happens to the water over time.

Discrepant Events for 5–8 Science

- **Motion and forces**
  Concept: Bernoulli's Principle — the faster the flow of a fluid, the lower the pressure it exerts.

(Continued)

> **Activity 1**
>
> Give each student a strip of paper (15 cm x 3 cm) and have each make a fold at one end of the paper about two cm from the end. Hold the strip by the folded end and blow against the underside of the paper. Observe what happens.
>
> Now have students place the fold against their bottom lip (thumb against chin) and ask students to predict what will happen when they blow across the top of the paper.
>
> Discuss: What do we know about stationary air? (It exerts equal pressure on all sides of an object.) What is different about the air we blow over the paper than the air that is under the paper? (The air above the strip is moving faster than the air below the strip.) What effect does the faster moving airflow have? (The paper is pushed upward because the faster moving air exerts less pressure on the paper strip than the stationary air below it.)
>
> Modified from T. L. Liem (1998)

School Site Investigations

Active involvement in worthwhile experiences creates awareness, generates questions, and stimulates the mind. The school site provides an environment for observing phenomena, organisms, and events related to content standards, and it provides space for creating human graphs and models of the solar system and for playing instructional games.

Firsthand observations of earth materials, such as rock outcrops or soil profiles, observations of the sun's position and shadows at different times of day, and observations of the moon at different times of the month generate questions and interest. In addition, students can observe changes in plants throughout the year, the effects of water and wind on the landscape, and the impact of humans and bus exhaust on vegetation.

School sites offer opportunities to conduct soil studies, "adopt" trees and investigate their unique characteristics, identify differences in the patterns of leaves and plants, make estimates or measure large objects, calculate area and perimeter, and explore the question, "how big is an acre"?

INFORMAL LEARNING ENVIRONMENTS

Many exciting and stimulating learning environments exist in the community. Informal learning environments offer firsthand opportunities for students to observe new and novel organisms, objects, and phenomena related to standards-based concepts and form mental images to enhance their understanding of concepts and skills.

For example, a great way to introduce young children to the many groups of animals beyond those that are familiar is to take them to the zoo and involve them in observations of the unique physical characteristics of the major groups of animals: mammals, birds, fish, reptiles, and amphibians.

Classification activities using pictures of animals can be done before the trip to assess prior knowledge and to introduce group names and characteristics and after the trip to reinforce and show understanding of content categories. Children may draw some of the animals they visit and classify them as part of the activity. The multisensory, kinesthetic experiences will aid in the development of mental models.

As with other strategies for activating and engaging, well-designed field experiences involve students in every step of the instructional process. Figure 25 identifies a number of informal learning environments and some of the inquiry questions that might be generated and investigated at each site.

Video Clips

Unusual or dynamic presentations can spark interest and generate questions. For example, short video clips of volcanic eruptions, tsunamis, earthquakes, or other natural phenomena or pictures of oil spills, air and water pollution, and other human-created conditions show how these happenings impact the lives of people living around them and, ultimately, all of us.

Video presentations, such as the New Explorers Series, provide realistic views of scientists and valuable insights into the ways scientists think and work. Middle school students can observe scientists in action and identify such things as the following:

- Science as a human, interdisciplinary endeavor.
- The questions and theories that drive the scientist's work.
- The procedures used to investigate phenomena.
- Types of technology that are useful to the scientist.
- Ways that scientists work cooperatively with members of a team and collaboratively with scientists from other countries.
- The contributions of the research to the welfare of humans and other living things.
- Costs and risks involved in conducting research.

Figure 25   Informal Learning Environments and Inquiry Questions

Informal Learning Environments	Inquiry Questions to Investigate
Zoo, Aquarium, Aviary; Animal Theme Park	• What are the characteristics of a certain group of animals? • What are the features of their habitats? What do they need for survival? • How are animals of the same species similar and different? • What adaptations do animals have that enable them to survive in their natural habitats? • What are some ways animals and plants are dependent on one another? • What are some animal food chains and food webs? • What do the stages in the life cycles of various animals look like? How are they alike and how are they different? • What are some interesting or unusual behaviors of animals? • What can I learn about animal behavior by observing animals "perform"?
Amusement Park	• What kinds of forces and motion will I observe or experience on a roller coaster or other ride? • What are the causes of the forces and motion? • What is the role of friction in various rides? • What simple machines make up complex machinery? How do the simple machines work together to enable machinery to function? • How does the technology apply principles of light, sound, and heat?
Museums	• How do specimens and models provide information about properties of objects and organisms? • How can firsthand interactions with and observations of specimens, such as rocks and minerals, animal skulls, pelts, fossils, artifacts, pendulums, simple machines, and others, enrich our understanding of them?
Technology Centers	• In what ways does technology apply the concepts and principles of science? • How can technology enhance data collection and storage, measurement, and visual displays? • How has technology changed over time? • What tools of technology can be used for solving problems and extending learning? • How does society depend on technology for energy, our water, and other resources?

Informal Learning Environments	Inquiry Questions to Investigate
School Site, Parks, Outdoor Education Centers, Nature Centers, Botanic Gardens, Farms, Seashore, Quarries, and Other Informal Science Centers	• What plants and animals are native to this environment? • What interactions between plants and animals can be observed? • What effects do the following natural phenomena have on the area: wind, waves, tornados, floods, earthquakes, or hurricanes? • What effects do human activities have on the natural environment? In what ways have they been helpful and what ways have they been harmful? • What can we learn by observation and investigation (e.g., hunting for fossils, observing and collecting rocks, observing animal behaviors, caring for animals, collecting sap and making maple syrup, and investigating fields, forests, ponds, lakes, or rivers)? • What does farm machinery look like and what does it do? • Where do milk products come from? How are meat-producing animals cared for? How are fruits and vegetables planted and harvested?

Guest Speakers

Scientists and other professionals can be invited to make relevant presentations. They often bring props to enhance their presentations such as animals that perform amazing feats, endangered species that have been rehabilitated, unusual rock and mineral specimens, or equipment to demonstrate physical science phenomena, stimulate emotions, and instill a sense of wonder in students. Often, presentations include student volunteers or engage the audience to further personalize the experience.

Displays

Health organizations or hospitals often have displays that are available to schools for short periods of time. For example, displays may show the structures and functioning of healthy and nonhealthy body systems and organs and identify factors such as smoking, poor dietary choices, or use of drugs that contribute to the unhealthy conditions. Such displays may provide realistic perspectives that effect students emotionally, causing concern and positive action.

Student groups may also create displays that affect the welfare of students in their schools, such as those related to safety in and out of school.

Literature in Science

The integration of science with mathematics, literature, and language arts provides a holistic approach to learning. Reading stories or poems can capture student interest and generate questions that can be answered through investigations or extended research. Annotated lists of outstanding science trade books for students K–12 are published annually by the Children's Book Council (www.cbcbooks.org) and the National Science Teachers Association (www.nsta.org). The titles are classified by topic and provide a wealth of information about each title. *Once Upon a GEMS Guide* (Barber et al., 1996), published by the Lawrence Hall of Science, offers an annotated bibliography of hundreds of books of stories and poems that link to GEMS Guides that are based on major science concepts. The AIMS Education Foundation (www.aimsedu.org) publishes books of concept-based activities that include lists of current topic-related trade books.

Case Studies

Case studies not only involve students in reading about issues related to science or the environment, but they provide opportunities for students to focus on the ways that scientists think and act. Students are given short articles or scenarios related to standards-based concepts to read individually or in small groups.

The popular press offers an abundance of short, newsworthy articles that can be used to enhance reading and promote the understanding of scientific inquiry. A news story about an environmental or ecological problem or issue related to a topic or concept can be analyzed as students investigate the science concept. Through this approach, students learn how scientists investigate and use technology to solve real-world problems by making observations, asking questions, hypothesizing, gathering data, and formulating theories. Students can also realize the "trade-offs" in terms of costs, risks, and benefits associated with a search for solutions to such problems.

Because not all articles reveal all aspects of scientific investigation, teachers may wish to identify the components of an inquiry that are described in the article and provide students with a template of headings to guide their reading. The guiding framework may include any number of headings that are appropriate, such as the following:

- Problem
- Observations
- Hypothesis
- Strategies for Investigation
- Findings
- Solutions

- News Steps or New Problems
- Others that "fit" the article

For example, the Associated Press reported a mysterious incident of elk die-offs in southern Wyoming that brought about a thorough investigation of its cause. Over 300 elk were found dead or dying in the Red Rim Wildlife Management Area in February 2004. The article described in detail the processes used by scientists to develop a theory to explain the problem.

The case study can be read, analyzed, and discussed as students study fungi, algae, and lichen, the integrated associations of algal cells tangled in a lattice of fungi, ecological succession, plant or animal adaptations, or food chains. In this case, a ground-dwelling lichen, *Parmelia molliuscula,* abundant in desert soil in Wyoming, was found to be the cause of the deaths. Elk that are native to the area were not affected by an acid that is found in the lichen. The elk that were affected migrated from Colorado and lacked a microorganism that neutralizes the acid. This unique adaptation might prompt further investigation by interested students.

A CASE STUDY FOR AN ENVIRONMENTAL PROBLEM FOR MIDDLE SCHOOL SCIENCE

BBC News recently offered an article titled "Hungry World 'Must Eat Less Meat,'" which describes the role of water use in food production and calls attention to future problems of malnutrition water shortages in a growing population (story from BBC News published August 16, 2004: http://news.bbc.co.uk/2/hi/science/nature/355942.stm).

Goals and standards: The article addresses several important standards from the NSES (National Research Council, 1996) for Grades 5 to 8 under the following headings: Abilities Necessary to Do Inquiry and Populations and Ecosystems.

Abilities Necessary to Do Inquiry:

- Identify questions that can be answered through scientific inquiry.
- Think critically and logically to make relationships between evidence and explanations.
- Recognize and analyze alternative explanations and predictions.
- Communicate scientific procedures and explanations (National Research Council, 1996, p. 145).

(Continued)

(Continued)

Populations and Ecosystems:

- A population consists of all individuals of a species that occur together at a given place and time. All populations living together and the physical factors with which they interact compose an ecosystem.
- The number of organisms an ecosystem can support depends on the resources available and abiotic factors, such as quantity of light and water, range of temperatures, and soil composition (National Research Council, 1996).

Figure 26 shows headings that might be given to students to help them analyze this article and summaries of information that can be found in the article.

Figure 26   Analysis of an Article

Heading	Summary
Problem	Experts at the World Water Week Conference warned that world water supplies will not be enough for future generations to enjoy the same diet that the Western world currently follows.
Observations	Malnutrition is a worldwide problem. It is estimated that over 800 million people are undernourished or lack a secure food supply and the population is growing. Feeding more people will take more water as well as food. Much of the world is running out of water for increased food production. Why? Animals fed on grain and grazing animals require more water than grain crops require to produce the same amount of food.
Hypothesis	The world will have to change its consumption patterns and reduce the amount of water needed for producing food.
Facts or Findings	A study of water use for food production revealed that • A kilogram of grain-fed beef requires at least 15 cubic meters of water to produce; • A kilogram of grass-fed lamb requires 10 cubic meters; • A kilogram of grain requires from less than one to three cubic meters.
Solutions	Find ways to decrease the demand for meat while continuing to provide consumers with healthy diets that are high in nutrients.
Suggestions for Next Steps	1. Educate society about the relationship between water use and food production. 2. Reduce the amount of water used for food production by reducing the demand for meat. 3. Create a problem-solution graphic organizer.

6 Strategies for Acquiring and Exploring

INQUIRY DEFINED

Strategies for acquiring and exploring include the many ways that students learn content and develop skills and dispositions. National and many state standards endorse inquiry as the primary approach for learning science. Inquiry models the ways that scientists think and act and enables students to develop an understating of what it means to "do" science.

What is inquiry? Inquiry is defined by the NSES as the following: "the diverse ways that scientists study the natural world and propose explanations based on the evidence derived from their work and as the activities used by students to formulate an understanding of the work that scientists do" (National Research Council, 1996).

As a multifaceted activity, inquiry involves the following:

- Making observations.
- Posing questions.
- Accessing and using relevant information.
- Planning and carrying out data-rich investigations.
- Using tools and technology to collect, analyze, and interpret data.
- Proposing answers, explanations, and predictions.
- Communicating findings.

Why do we use it? Inquiry is an intellectual process for verifying answers to questions and explanations about natural objects, events, and phenomena. The inquiry process fosters the use of critical thinking as well as logic and reasoning skills. A full inquiry involves asking a question, planning and conducting an investigation, using equipment and tools to gather data, analyzing and interpreting data, using evidence to formulate a conclusion, and communicating the process, explanations, and results. Through an inquiry approach, students develop skills for acquiring knowledge, develop thinking and reasoning skills, apply scientific ideas and understandings, and communicate information in meaningful ways. Allowing students to ask and answer their own questions is just another way to differentiate learning.

What does it look like? Inquiry-based activities are not all alike. We may view them on a continuum ranging from those that are very structured to those that are less structured or "ill-structured" (see Figure 27).

Figure 28 provides a basic description for each type of inquiry.

TRADITIONAL VERSUS INQUIRY-BASED CLASSROOMS

The inquiry classroom may be viewed in terms of a set of teacher and student behaviors or the nature of student work. As a student-centered environment, the inquiry classroom provides both the setting and opportunities for teachers to apply a variety of methods and strategies for differentiating instruction to meet the needs of all students.

Figure 29 shows the characteristics of the traditional classroom and the inquiry classroom in terms of teacher behaviors, student learning, and student work.

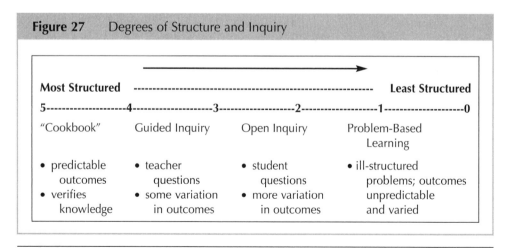

Figure 27   Degrees of Structure and Inquiry

Most Structured			Least Structured
5--------4--------3--------2--------1--------0			
"Cookbook"	Guided Inquiry	Open Inquiry	Problem-Based Learning
• predictable outcomes • verifies knowledge	• teacher questions • some variation in outcomes	• student questions • more variation in outcomes	• ill-structured problems; outcomes unpredictable and varied

SOURCE: Modified from Hammerman (2006a)

Figure 28	Types of Inquiry

Lesson Type	Description
Highly Structured "Cookbook"	A precise set of steps with predictable outcomes; activities are like "recipes" showing steps to be followed for collecting prescribed data; little critical or creative thinking involved; often used to merely verify content.
Guided Inquiry	Generally allows for a variety of approaches and variations in data; based on teacher- or student-generated questions followed by one or more activities, data collecting opportunities, and thought-provoking and reflective questions through which students develop new insights and understandings; often followed by a set of new questions that prompt further, more open investigations.
Open Inquiry	Implies a less formal structure for dealing with teacher- or student-generated questions; may be based on such things as • Observations or interest; • Activities or experiences; • Real-world problems; • Defense of a position.
Problem-Based Learning (PBL)	Least structured type of inquiry; students investigate teacher- or student-generated ill-structured problems through a variety of pathways, often determined by students. For example, students might be presented with a problem such as where to place power lines in a developing community or how to deal with endangered species in their community.

FACTORS THAT SUPPORT INQUIRY AND DIFFERENTIATED INSTRUCTION IN SCIENCE

High quality instruction requires adequate time, space, equipment, and resources necessary to engage students in multisensory, challenging investigations and experiences. To apply differentiated instructional strategies, it is critical to have a supportive environment, appropriate equipment and supplies, and a well-managed classroom.

Environments That Support Inquiry-Based Teaching and Learning

School systems that support inquiry-based teaching and learning provide the following policies, practices, and resources (see page 87):

Figure 29 Traditional Versus Inquiry Science Classrooms

Traditional Classroom	Inquiry Classroom
Teacher Behaviors	**Teacher Behaviors**
Expository method dominates; "teach is tell" mentality; test preparation is major focus	Uses a variety of methods and strategies to investigate and analyze questions and address standards
Directs all activities for students; uses a "cook book"—1 right answer approach	Allows students to ask questions and design activities; mediates and monitors learning
Tells students what they will learn; explains the concepts and relationships	Facilitates student thinking; allows students to explain concepts; uses "wait time" in questioning
Uses same content every year	Learns with students; revises content and approaches based on student achievement data
Uses text and video for content and verification of concepts	Uses a variety of resources; provides a meaningful context for engaged learning
Instruction focused on "right answers" with minimal relevance or application to real world	Instruction guides students to concept and skill development and varied applications to selves, their community, and the world
Student As Passive Receiver	**Student As Active Learner**
Listens to lectures or takes notes	Records data, processes information, and builds understanding
Memorizes terms and facts	Uses terms and facts to describe, interpret, and communicate
Follows teacher or worksheet directions with no deviation	Designs activities, research, and investigations to answer questions
Regards teacher as authority	Shares responsibility for learning; self-assesses
Student Work—Prescribed	**Student Work—Varied**
Emphasis on notes, worksheets, or end of chapter questions	Emphasis on investigations, student-generated data, research, and meaning
All students complete same tasks; "canned" labs	Tasks vary; investigations are "real world" with emphasis on data and research

Traditional Classroom	Inquiry Classroom
Student Work—Prescribed	**Student Work—Varied**
Teacher directs all tasks	Teacher and students direct tasks
Shows little or no thinking or reasoning, problem solving, or explanations	Shows evidence of thinking, reasoning, problem solving, explanations, and research
Little or no use of visuals to show understanding or relationships	Uses visuals to show and describe understanding and relationships

SOURCE: Modified from Hammerman (2006c)

- Rigid policies that endorse safety.
- Flexible scheduling.
- Books, models, visuals, and technological resources.
- Adequate supply of equipment and manipulative materials and funds for replacement of consumable materials.
- Appropriate technology and training in the use of technology.
- Strong administrative support.
- Ongoing professional development for teachers.

Classroom Features

Most traditional classrooms can be arranged and equipped to accommodate inquiry activities. Needs will vary with the grade and ability levels of students and the nature of the activities. Some classroom features that will enable teachers to differentiate instruction are as follows:

- Flat desks or tables that allow two to four students to work together.
- Sinks and availability of fresh water.
- First aid kits, safety goggles, rubber gloves, and other safety equipment.
- Separate tables or shelves for equipment, books, and resources.
- Space for students to work on individual or small group projects.
- Space and tables or counters for centers for relearning or extended learning.

- Computers, software, and Internet access; areas for use of technology, such as video equipment and microscopes.
- Tables or shelves for displaying products such as mobiles and models; wall space to display posters and drawings and timelines.
- Word walls or posters for key vocabulary words to reinforce spelling and to prompt students to use appropriate scientific vocabulary when writing and speaking.

Equipment and Supplies

Multisensory learning requires equipment and materials that enable students to investigate and develop standards-based concepts, construct understandings, and apply learning to solve problems. Often budgetary decisions are made by administrators who do not comprehend the importance of having the equipment and materials that are needed for hands-on, inquiry-based instruction. School systems that value science education will have an adequate budget for equipment and consumable materials for every grade level.

Management Strategies

An atmosphere of trust and cooperation that embraces empathy and risk-taking promotes healthy relationships between and among students and provides a setting for differentiated learning to occur. In such environments, students share responsibility for learning, enabling them to build on their strengths, learn by their mistakes, and use traditional and alternative pathways for reaching educational goals.

Much can be said about classroom management and factors that influence student motivation and behavior, and some important considerations will be offered throughout this text. Students should have input into establishing classroom "rules" and expectations for behavior and understand how these will enable them to enjoy flexibility throughout the learning process. A well organized, student-centered classroom that offers challenging instruction, flexible grouping and assignments, and a positive approach to learning will enable students to reach their full potential.

GUIDED INQUIRY LESSON FOR THE INTERMEDIATE LEVEL: INVESTIGATING WATER EROSION

Content: Waves, Wind, Water, and Ice Shape and Reshape Earth's Land Surface

Investigating Water Erosion

Background and Description of Activity

Waves, wind, water, and ice shape and reshape the Earth's land surface. Water is a powerful force that affects the landscape, especially on steep slopes, such as hillsides and mountainous areas, and where the land is not protected by vegetation, such as beaches.

Students will investigate water as an agent of erosion by:

1. Observing the effects of erosion in their environment;

2. Comparing the effects of water on bare soil versus soil with plants;

3. Identifying areas of their community and their state where water causes erosion and landslides. Students will apply their learning to their environment and to the decisions people make about where they will live—on hillsides, in mountainous areas, and along seashores—and identify risks that are associated with their choices.

Standards and Objectives

Following this activity, students will

- Explain how moving water can change the features of the landscape;
- Explain the difference in the way(s) water affects soil erosion on a barren hillside versus a hillside with vegetation;
- Explain the cause-and-effect relationships associated with moving water on the landscape (hillsides, mountains, beaches, farm land, and so forth) in their community and state;
- Make recommendations for minimizing the effects of erosion;
- Describe the risks when people choose to live in erosion-prone areas.

Materials

For each group of four students provide the following: an aluminum tray, sand or soil, syringe or spray bottle, graduated cylinder, access to water, paper towels, and notebooks.

Provide instructions for the investigation.

Engage and Explore

Read *The Mountain That Loved a Bird* (McLerran,1985) to show the interrelationships between the living and nonliving components of the environment.

Define erosion: Show pictures or video clips to introduce erosion as a natural process that changes the surface of the Earth. The agents of erosion are waves, wind, water, and ice.

Inquiry Question No. 1: In what ways does water affect the landscape?

1. Do a K-W-L to find out what students know and identify any misconceptions.

2. Take students on a "'school-site field trip" to find examples of water erosion. Record data or make drawings in notebooks (areas where puddles form, where soil or sand has been washed away, where natural streams form, etc.).

3. Discuss findings and answer Inquiry Question No. 1.

4. Allow students to generate questions for further investigation.

Acquire and Explore

Inquiry Question No. 2: How does moving water affect a barren hillside, a hillside with rocks and gravel, and a hillside with vegetation?

Each student should make and record predictions in notebooks.

(Continued)

Investigating Water Erosion (Continued)

Divide students into groups of four; provide each group with materials and instructions for the investigation. Students within each group may be assigned roles or determine their own roles.

1. Create a small hill of loose sand or soil on one end of a metal tray. Raise the hill end of the tray using a brick or several books. Measure and fill syringes or spray bottles with water (measure volume in cc or ml). Make a data table for recording observations. Sprinkle water on the sand or soil. Observe and record. Repeat several times. Record.

2. Recreate the hill of sand or soil. Place pebbles or small rocks on the "hill." Repeat No. 1. Observe and record.

3. Recreate the mound of sand or soil. Place a piece of sod on the hillside. Repeat No. 1. Observe and record.

Explain and Apply Learning; Create Meaning

Design a set of questions appropriate to the investigations for processing data, creating meaning, and making connections; for example:

1. Describe and discuss findings for tests 1 to 3. Answer inquiry question. Compare your findings to your original predictions. Were they similar or different? If different, why do you think so?

2. Discuss the effects of soil texture and vegetation on erosion and the reshaping of landscape.

3. Draw conclusions about the effects of water on various types of landscapes—such as unprotected beaches (introduce waves and show pictures of large waves or destruction from tsunamis), unprotected hillsides or mountains with little vegetation, hillsides with vegetation, landscapes with little slope. Introduce mudslides. Show pictures of landslides.

4. Identify mountains, seashores, or hilly areas in your state where people live. Locate these areas on a map. Identify and discuss the risks and consequences of living in areas that are affected by water erosion.

5. What are some ways to prevent soil erosion?

Elaborate and Extend

1. Find out what happens to rich agricultural soil on hillsides when crops are harvested. Where does it go? What are some ways to minimize the loss of valuable soil?

2. What are tsunamis? Where do they occur? What types of damage results from tsunamis? What are some ways tsunamis can be predicted or prevented?

3. What causes beaches to be eroded? How can eroded beaches be reclaimed?

Assess and Evaluate

Use discussion, notebook entries, written explanations, and a teacher-designed quiz to determine if students

- Know how moving water can change the features of the landscape;
- Can show data and explain how water affects soil erosion on a barren hillside versus a hillside with vegetation;
- Can give an example of a cause-and-effect relationship associated with moving water on the landscape in their community and state;
- Know ways to minimize the effects of erosion;
- Are able to describe the risks associated with living in erosion-prone areas.

Support for English Learners

The outdoor investigation at the beginning of the project will "operationally define" the concept of erosion for all students and especially the English Language learners.

Language learners should team with English-speaking students in the classroom group so that the English-speaking students can assist with recording observations, completing data tables, and answering questions.

PROBLEM-BASED LEARNING

What is it? Problem-based learning (PBL) is an approach to learning where instruction is designed around real-world, relevant problems. Students are presented with a problem and, through a series of investigations and activities, they learn concepts, practice skills of learning, and explore solutions to the problem. Teachers serve as facilitators, coaching student thinking and guiding student inquiry.

Why do we use it? PBL is a unique and novel way to address curricular goals and standards. Through this approach, teachers decide on ways to frame student involvement in a problem that is related to them or to their community and provide opportunities for students to research solutions to the problem. Solutions to problems will vary, enabling students to view them from different perspectives, thus more globally. For example, when studying an environmental problem, students may select one of several perspectives from which to view it, such as that of a legislator, an environmentalist, a home owner, a consumer, a business owner, or a worker.

What does it look like? Instruction designed around ill-structured problems does the following:

- Engages students as stakeholders.
- Provides a relevant context for learning.
- Fosters thinking and problem solving.
- Leads to deep understanding of related concepts.

PBL has two components: problem design and problem implementation. Creating and implementing a unit of instruction using PBL includes the following:

- Choosing a relevant problem.
- Developing the learning adventure.
- Building the teaching and learning template.
- Preparing and engaging the students.
- Coaching critical thinking and learning events toward generating solutions.
- Embedding periodic assessments and appropriate instruction.
- Debriefing the problem (Torp & Sage, 1998).

Examples of PBL Topics

Every community has problems and issues that concern the citizens of that community, and there are many science concepts embedded within these social and environmental issues. PBL units have been designed around such topics as the following:

- Energy availability and usage within a growing community.
- Mounting wastes and locations of waste disposal sites.
- The benefits and risks of nuclear power plants versus other sources of energy.
- Issues related to use of public lands, including national parks.
- Protective measures for habitats of endangered species.
- Occurrences and causes of illness and birth defects.
- Toxic waste spills.

PROJECTS

What are they? Projects are in-depth studies of particular concepts, products, or applications. Projects usually relate to a particular subject area and have a specific focus. They are rich with opportunities for engaging learners and for developing deep understanding at a variety of levels of readiness or interest. Through projects, students are able to explore concepts as investigators and researchers of knowledge and create new or novel products through which they can show or describe understanding. Students often give presentations to share their learning.

Why do we use them? Projects are used because they build on students' interest and satisfy curiosity. Students learn to plan their time and develop their research skills at various levels. Projects provide students with choices, ownership, and responsibility. They encourage independence and self-directed learning skills and allow students to work at complex and abstract levels that match their skill level while managing time and materials. Projects are highly motivating and allow for in-depth work on interesting topics. Projects allow students to work at their own rate. However, they must be worth the academic time of the learner and be meaningful experiences, not just time fillers.

Information learned in context with an emotional hook will be remembered longer if it is also a meaningful experience. Projects help the learner to interact with knowledge at a level higher than simple recall and they emphasize process as well as product. They integrate concepts with skills and help develop a deeper level of concept understanding. Projects enable students to construct understanding in a way that is meaningful for them.

What do they look like? Projects may or may not include the development of a product, but often models, brochures, posters, dioramas, plays, songs, or other products are created to show learning.

All projects should be designed with the end in mind, that is, projects should align with learning goals, standards, and content objectives. Projects should be appropriate for the age and ability levels of students so the work is interesting and challenging without being overwhelming.

Projects can be assigned or chosen by students from a choice list or board. When developing a list of projects, it is important to make sure that each choice meets certain criteria that correspond to specific learning goals. Criteria for projects will vary, but generally include the following:

- Ability level tasks that allows for independent or group work.
- A focus on important concepts or principles of science.
- A set of reasonable parameters.
- Emphasis on novelty and creativity.
- An established timeline.
- A clear description of requirements and the plan for assessment.
- A rubric for self-assessment.

Models

What are they? Models are three-dimensional representations designed to show the structure or workings of an object, system, or concept.

Why do we use them? Models are powerful tools for learning since they enable students to observe characteristics of things that are not readily visible to them. Models of human body systems or organs, the ocean floor, the solar system, airplanes and rockets, and atoms are just a few of the many models that are available for classroom use.

Building models is a great way to engage students in worthwhile learning. To build a model, students need to focus on significant details of a structure and its component parts including their shapes, sizes, positions, and relationships to other parts. Students enjoy engaging in projects that allow them to apply and reinforce concepts in meaningful ways. Model building requires students to manipulate materials, focus on detail, and use critical and creative thinking.

What do they look like? Primary students often make models to show the structures of living and nonliving things, such as animals, plants, rocks and soil, fossils, the sun and earth, or habitats. Student-created models of cells, body systems and organs, the earth, the solar system, oceans, volcanoes, folding and faulting, atoms and molecules, and simple machines are commonly found in intermediate and middle grade classrooms.

Likewise, student-made collections of bones, insects, feathers, flowers, leaves, seeds, rocks and minerals, and gliders show evidence of active learning.

Booklets, Posters, and Brochures

Projects may take the form of posters, brochures, or booklets. Such projects may involve students in library or Internet research to gather information. Posters, brochures, or booklets may be designed to do the following:

- Trace the history of a theory or invention.
- Show or apply concepts in a new or novel way.
- Describe a problem and suggest solutions.
- Apply concepts.

Projects at the Primary, Intermediate, and Middle Grade Levels

Primary level: As part of a unit on life cycles of organisms, students might create a booklet with drawings of the various stages in the life cycle of the darkling beetle. The booklet may include explanations and drawings related to various investigations they conduct with mealworms (the larva stage) including tests for behavior and movement and tests for their preferences for a light or dark environment, a wet or dry environment, and types of food. Students can display their booklets and explain their understanding of the behavior of organisms and the life cycle of the darkling beetle. As an extension, they can compare the life cycle of this organism with the life cycles of other insects.

Intermediate level: As part of a unit on earth materials, students might make posters showing the rock cycle, ways minerals are used in their homes, in school, and in the community, or the importance of minerals such as calcium, iron, and others in a well-balanced diet.

Middle grade level: As part of a unit on forces and motion, students will create a brochure that shows an early science-related invention, such as the printing press or the microscope. The brochure should include the following:

1. Drawings of the invention and the inventor.

2. Information about the inventor.

3. History of the invention.

4. Labeling of the simple machines that were used in the construction of the early invention.

Students will present their brochures to the class or to small groups. They will describe each of the simple machines they identified and tell how each functioned in the invention.

PROJECT CHOICES FOR A UNIT ON CELLS

Students might work on projects during a unit of instruction. For example, the following list of projects might be offered for students to work on individually or with a partner during a unit titled "The Cell":

1. **Whole Cell Catalog:** Create a catalog for something for which there may not yet be a market, such as the major organelles in a cell. Create catalog pages to sell two of the major organelles.

2. **Edible Cell:** Construct a cell model using edible materials to represent the cell and its major organelles. For example, bake a cake with different types of candies to represent each organelle.

3. **Journey Into the Cell:** Write and illustrate a creative story similar to *The Magic School Bus* series where people and animals are miniaturized and traveling inside and around cells.

4. **Infomercial About the Cell:** Script, direct, tape, and edit a commercial to explain the major organelles of a cell.

5. **PowerPoint on the Cell:** Create a PowerPoint presentation that summarizes the structure and function of the major organelles of a cell.

6. **Cell Poster:** Design and create a giant poster showing the major organelles of the cell. Display your work.

7. **3-D Model of the Cell:** Design and create a three-dimensional model of the cell showing the major organelles.

Science Fair Projects

Science fair projects often must be controlled experiments. These require students to identify inquiry questions that require them to test one variable for its effect on another while controlling all other conditions. For example, students may conduct three experiments to determine whether the period of a pendulum (number of swings per minute) is affected by (a) a change in the weight of a pendulum bob, (b) a change in the amplitude of the pendulum, or (c) a change in the length of the pendulum.

Sample Projects

Young students may conduct experiments to determine the effects of polluted water or salt water, music, nutrients, amount or type of light, or other factors on the growth of plants. Intermediate or middle grade students might test various colors of paper or cloth to see which color absorbs the most heat when exposed to the sun over time. They may test to see if water cycles more quickly in a warm environment or experiment to find out what effect heat has on the dissolving rates of sugar, salt, or other solutes.

Besides being a great way to build concept understanding, experiments are rich with process and thinking skills. In planning and conducting controlled experiments, students will do the following:

- Make observations.
- Access and use relevant information about things they want to study.
- Ask questions about the effect of one variable on another.
- State a hypothesis to describe a plausible relationship between variables.
- Design an action plan to test the hypothesis.
- Identify and select appropriate materials and equipment.
- Design and use a data table to record data and observations.
- Conduct the experiment and control variables.
- Make a graph or use a graphic organizer to display data.
- Draw conclusions.
- Summarize conclusions and any problems encountered.
- Suggest changes in the procedures, as needed.
- Repeat the experiment, if necessary.
- Communicate, describe, and apply learning.

Product Testing and Survey Research

Some projects fall under the categories of product testing or survey research. In these types of projects, students might do the following:

- Design and conduct tests of wet strength and absorbency with consideration of cost to determine which brand of paper towel (or other paper product) is the "best buy."
- Test products to see how well they hold up to their "claims."
- Survey students in their class to determine favorite music, snacks, sports, or movies.
- Offer various types of foods to cats, gerbils, lizards, or mice to identify food preferences.
- Collect weather data over time or make observations of the moon to identify patterns in nature.
- Survey students or adults to gather data about product use, beliefs, or behaviors.

Although these types of studies are not controlled experiments, they do provide opportunities for young students to ask questions, design and carry out action plans, and collect data to answer their questions.

Science and Technological Design

Projects that link science and technological design, such as building and testing structures, designing new inventions, creating insulators, making improvements on existing products, or applying concepts to solve problems require students to draw on their knowledge and skills yet challenge them to explore new avenues of creativity and critical thinking.

For example, a middle school class looked at developing innovative products that would be useful to the elderly in the community. Through the project, students applied and developed literacy skills as they created questionnaires, surveys, and interviews to gather data from the elderly. They used the Internet to access information on trends and needs. They applied principles of physical science, technology, and mathematics to the design of their innovative products. They drew their designs and displayed them. Students from other classes visited their "product gallery" where designers described their work and answered questions about how they applied the principles of physical science.

PRESENTATIONS

What are they and why do we use them? Presentations are ways that students organize information, use technology, and communicate ideas and information to others.

What do they look like? Effective presentations often include the use of visuals such as models, pictures, posters, or PowerPoint slides. A presentation may include a demonstration or engage the audience in an activity. Teachers or students may wish to design a rubric to guide in the design and delivery of the presentation.

STATIONS

What are they? Stations are separate places around the classroom, lab, or other instructional area where different but topic-related activities are set up. The stations generally have equipment, materials, and a set of directions for performing the task.

Why are they used? Stations are an excellent way to engage students in active learning. Through this approach, many of the intelligences can be tapped, since each station generally has a different focus or requirement. Stations involve students physically and mentally in their learning.

Stations maximize the use of equipment and materials. For example, in a classroom of 24 students where there are only four balances and mass sets available, four stations can be set up with tasks requiring the use of a balance and mass set. As students rotate among stations as individuals or pairs, they can have hands-on experiences with the equipment four times rather than working in a group of six and having minimal firsthand experience. Sometimes there may be only one piece of equipment available to students, such as a model skeleton or a telescope. Using the item at a station would enable each student to interact with it to answer a question or solve a problem.

What do they look like? Stations will vary with the types of tasks, but generally each has a set of materials and a set of directions for the task that is to be accomplished. Each task should have a worthwhile purpose related to the development or application of a concept, development of skills, or both. Work done at each station may be recorded in a notebook, or data sheets may be provided at each station. Tasks may require students to work cooperatively, manipulate materials and use tools of technology, make and record observations, collect data, use numbers, make drawings or models, apply concepts, and summarize learning. Observation checklists, data sheets or notebook entries, demonstrations of knowledge or ability, and formal and nonformal discussion can be used to assess work at stations.

Examples of Stations at the Primary Grade Level

For a unit on properties of matter, stations may be set up with opportunities for students to discover properties of solids, liquids, and gases. Following are examples of some of the tasks that may be included:

- Identify color, size, shape, texture, weight, and other properties for sets of solid objects.
- Classify a set of objects as being made of metal, plastic, or wood.
- Classify a set of objects by observable properties, draw the subsets, and describe the plan.
- Serial order objects by size, shape, color, and texture.
- Sort a set of objects by their magnetic properties (magnetic and nonmagnetic), describe how magnets are used in your home (refrigerator magnets, clasps on handbags, magnets in stuffed animals and other toys).

- Investigate properties of water: pour water into different size containers and observe how the same amount changes in appearance; change properties of water by mixing it with soluble materials (water + food dye = new color; water + sugar = "sticky" water).
- Float objects in plain water and in salt water and then make a comparison.
- Find the mass of two ice cubes in a small baggie, label the bag, and return to the station later in the day to find the mass of the melted ice cubes in the baggie.
- Take a flat plastic bag and whirl it around until it is "puffed up." Blow up a balloon, then observe the balloon as the air leaves it. Summarize how you know that air takes up space.
- Play a game with a set of buttons: one partner sorts the buttons by a property and the other partner tries to guess the property.

Example of Stations at the Intermediate Grade Level

Stations work well for providing practice in developing understanding of and skill in using the metric system. A variety of tasks providing opportunities for students to measure distance, mass, volume, and temperature in metric units can be set up at various stations. Working in small cooperative groups, students rotate among the stations. Tasks should be designed so that students perform each task at each station and record their data on data sheets or in notebooks that can be used as part of formative assessment. Teachers move among groups to observe student behavior, use of equipment, understanding of tasks and concepts, and problem-solving ability. Teachers can monitor student progress through questioning and dialog and offer additional challenges for groups that complete the task early (see Mini Metric Olympics in Campopiano et al., 1987).

Example of Stations at the Middle Grade Level

When students are being introduced to the use of equipment for observing minute detail in living and nonliving things, stations provide a way to introduce various types of equipment, such as magnifiers and microscopes or computer-based microscopes to observe details on prepared slides and wet mounts of organisms, such as insects and single-celled organisms, parts of organisms, such as muscle or blood cells and plant parts, and other natural objects, such as feathers and rocks.

If students are studying a particular topic, such as the types and structures of human body cells and tissues, the stations can be set up to show how the different types or powers of equipment enable them to learn more about the topic. For example, each station can provide one or more microscopic views of muscle, bone, blood, nerve, and other human body cells and tissues under high and low power to enable students to compare similarities and differences. They can compare their images of cells with those offered through software and Internet sites.

CENTERS

What are they? Like stations, centers are instructional spaces set up to provide students with specific experiences for learning or relearning concepts, extending learning, developing skills, exploring interests, or providing challenges in a topic area. At centers, students can explore new avenues of learning and have the freedom to work on tasks at their own pace.

Why do we use them? Centers provide opportunities for learners to do the following:

- Remediate, enhance, or extend knowledge of concepts.
- Explore connections, applications, and careers.
- Pursue interests and explore new ways of knowing.
- Practice skills and valued dispositions.
- Be challenged at their ability level.
- Solve problems and invent new products or strategies.
- Make choices and work at their own pace.
- Manipulate different types of materials.
- Apply complex thinking processes and promote the growth of dendrites.

What do they look like? Centers are places where the work can be made to fit the learner's needs, ranging from basic learning to remediation to enrichment. As such, centers are an ideal design for adjustable assignments. Centers may be structured or exploratory in nature and can be set up in different ways. Establishing centers facilitates many diverse opportunities for learning to take place.

Teachers can consciously adjust activities for the centers in the planning process and assign appropriate learners to the various centers. By having a variety of materials and tasks at one station, students become more responsible for their learning. They make choices and set their own learning goals. There is an intrinsic reward for self-achievement.

Structured Centers

A structured center has specific tasks assigned and an agenda developed by the teacher. During center time, students work with skills or concepts, approaching them through a variety of experiences. Multilevel tasks are designed to develop a certain skill or concept in this type of center. During center time, students work at their level of need and at their own pace while being challenged with complex, hands-on learning (see Chapman & Freeman, 1996).

Exploratory Centers

An exploratory center has materials or resources provided and allows the student to decide what to do with those materials. For example, the center might provide a variety of fiction and nonfiction reading materials on a particular topic. The student decides which material to read and how long to read. A student settles down to read a selection because of a high interest in the topic and an appropriate reading level (see Chapman & Freeman, 1996).

Relearning Centers

Centers may be set up for relearning important concepts and skills, enhancing understanding, or extending learning. They may provide materials and resources for students to design and conduct experiments to answer their questions. Some of the different types of centers that can be designed for science are as follows:

- Topic or theme centers that provide hands-on learning activities in a topic area with different levels of difficulty.
- Interest centers that provide enrichment activities for further investigation of a topic.
- Free choice centers that provide activities for experimenting, discovering, and inventing.
- Computer-based learning centers with multimedia resources for supplemental or remedial use.
- Resource centers with a wide variety of reading materials for relearning or extended learning.
- Art centers with a media table to create artifacts such as models, technological designs, or new inventions.
- Skills centers for practice of important skills.
- Project centers with writing and drawing tools and various types and sizes of paper for creating newspapers, brochures, booklets, posters, letters, articles, or poems.
- Challenge centers for problem solving.
- Listening centers with music or readings from both fictional and factual content.

ASSESSMENT FOR STATIONS AND CENTERS

Students need to be accountable for the work they do at stations and centers. Students should keep detailed records of processes, information, data, answers to inquiry questions, and summaries of learning in notebooks or on data sheets that are provided at each station or center.

Assessments should relate directly to the concept, process, and disposition-related goals and objectives of the unit or area of study. Students should be aware of instructional goals and objectives for their study, and a rubric should be developed by the teacher (with input from students) to guide instruction and allow for student self-assessment. See Chapter 9 for information on alignment and rubric designs.

As teachers visit stations and centers and interact with students, they may use the following:

- Observation checklists to gather information related to procedures, skills, and behaviors.
- Informal questioning to determine concept understanding.
- Notebook entries to monitor progress.

In addition, periodic quizzes related to key concepts will provide information needed to guide instruction and "next steps" for individual students or teams.

USING STATIONS AND CENTERS IN MIDDLE SCHOOL SCIENCE: INVESTIGATING EARTH HISTORY

As part of a unit on earth history, Mr. Marshall, a middle school science teacher, used two fossil activity kits (such as those available through Creative Dimensions, P.O. Box 1393, Bellingham, WA 98227) supplemented with additional fossils to introduce his students to the geologic timeline and some of the plants and animals that existed throughout geologic history. Fifteen stations were set up around the classroom, each with two copies of an activity card that shows the geologic timeline, the age of the fossil and its origin, magnifiers, and other materials needed for students to investigate the fossils.

Activate and engage: Mr. Marshall introduced the topic by asking students what they knew about geologic time and fossils. Students generated and recorded a list of questions based on what they did and did not know. Inquiry questions included the following:

1. What are fossils and how are they formed?

2. How do fossils provide evidence of life in the past?

3. How are fossils similar to and different from organisms that exist today?

4. How do the types and ages of fossils provide information about conditions on the earth during geologic time?

Mr. Marshall introduced a collection of fossils which students observed. They noted properties and ages of the fossils and ordered them by age on a large geologic timeline at the front of the classroom. Recalling the set of inquiry questions, Mr. Marshall invited students to investigate fossils by working at 15 different stations with a partner throughout the week and completing the tasks at each station.

Acquire and explore: Students worked with partners and rotated among the stations in specified time periods throughout the week. Each station had one to four investigations or thought-provoking questions that involved the students in using the same processes paleontologists use to learn about life in the past. As they investigated the assortment of fossils, students made observations, classified, measured and estimated, determined density, tested for physical and chemical properties, made inferences, compared and contrasted, recorded and communicated data, summarized learning, and used other process and thinking skills. Students made fossil notebooks to record activities and information from each station. Their notebook entries included descriptions of organisms and investigations, data tables and data, labeled drawings, and summaries of learning.

Explain and apply: Following the investigations, students engaged in a discussion of processes, findings, and meaning. They shared information and data from each station and traced the ages of their newly discovered organisms through the geologic timeline. Students generated new questions and topics for further research and investigation.

Elaborate and extend—Centers for relearning and extended learning: Following the week of study, centers equipped with materials and resources were set up for students to do the following:

• Revisit, reinvestigate, and relearn important concepts or processes from week one.

(Continued)

(Continued)

> - Extend learning by investigating new questions or topics through hands-on activities, resources, or computer programs or the Internet.
> - Engage in projects or studies involving reading, writing, music, art, or model building.
>
> *Assess and evaluate:* Student notebook entries, observed performances, use of tools and equipment, explanations, and informal dialog between students and between students and teacher provided continuous feedback on student progress throughout the week. At the end of the week, a teacher-made test based on specific objectives of the learning task assessed knowledge and understanding of the geologic timeline and some of the plants and animals that existed throughout geologic history.

CHOICE BOARDS

What are they? Choice boards are visual displays from which students can select one or more ways of processing information or rehearsing content or skills. Students may work alone or with one or more partners to accomplish the tasks they select.

Why do we use them? Choice boards allow students to select one or more activities for obtaining and sharing information. They offer students a variety of ways to learn more about or reinforce a concept, develop important skills, apply learning, or expand meaning. Choices designed around learning styles or multiple intelligences offer ways for students to capitalize on preferred approaches for learning and may be used to guide students to resources for extending learning.

What do they look like? Choice boards may be shown in a variety of formats and developed around topics that extend learning, learning styles, or multiple intelligences. What is most important is that they offer choices for learning important concepts and developing skills and dispositions.

Choice boards may be offered following a set of hands-on, investigative anchor or all-group activities that introduce and develop a basic understanding of content. The choices that follow the investigative activities may allow students to develop a deeper understanding of the concept, practice process, and thinking skills through additional investigations or application of concepts in meaningful ways or by exploring career areas.

Choice Boards for a Primary Level Study of Animals

The sample choice board in Figure 30 is a "tic-tac-toe" board where students are challenged to select three activities horizontally, vertically, or diagonally to achieve their goal. If students select a horizontal or diagonal row that includes the "wild card," they may design a research project of their choice.

CONTRACTS

What are they? Contracts (Berte, 1975; Knowles, 1986; Robbins, Gregory, & Herndon, 2000; Tomlinson, 1998a, 1999; Winebrenner, 1992) have often been used to allow students some flexibility and choice in their learning. Contracts have the potential for students to develop "flow," the state in which they are totally engaged in a challenging and motivating task that matches their skills and preferences.

Contracts provide students with clear goals and expectations for learning, choices for approaches to learning, ownership of their learning, and responsibility for managing time and tasks. When teachers set up a contract they need to consider the instructional goals and standards that will be targeted and the materials and resources that will be needed to accomplish the goals. Assessment tools, timelines, and clear expectations should be identified up front.

For example, for an intermediate grade unit on rocks and minerals, some students may be offered options for learning important concepts in ways that will motivate and interest them. Students may choose to participate in all or part of the classroom instruction and opt for other or additional activities or experiences.

Teacher and students work together to develop a contract that includes the following:

- Clear learning goals.
- A list of concepts to be learned.
- An action plan describing what the student will do.
- A timeline for completing the tasks.
- The resources and materials the student will need to accomplish the tasks.
- How learning will be assessed.

Assessments may be in the form of a written report, a project, a demonstration or a presentation, a blueprint, plan, or other visual, or a combination of these.

Contract for Rocks and Minerals

A sample outline and a sample contract are provided in Figures 31 and 32.

Figure 30   Choice Board for the Study of Animals

Research animals, such as the penguins or zebras that came from other countries. Explore the distribution of an animal group throughout the world. Create a comic book or pop-up book featuring your animal.	Make finger puppets of an animal in various stages of its life cycle. Write and perform a play that includes information about the animal, its habitat, and its life cycle.	Adopt a mealworm: Research and design a habitat for mealworms and observe them. Design a set of investigations to determine if they prefer light or dark or wet or dry environments. Observe the changes in the mealworms over time. Explain findings.
Create a shoebox diorama for an animal or animal group showing the animals in their habitat. Research factors of the environment that support or threaten their survival. Present findings.	**Wild Card** **Design an action research project to learn about a local animal or animals in one or more stages of their life cycles in your environment.** *For example:* *Find out when bird counts or other estimates of animal populations are being done in your community and get involved.* *Identify endangered species in your area and identify strategies for ensuring their survival. Create a poster with drawings to encourage people to help save the endangered organisms.*	Interview an animal breeder or trainer about inherited and learned behaviors of animals. Compare inherited and learned behaviors of animals at various stages in their life cycles and compare them to human behaviors.
Make a model or poster showing your favorite animal or your pet in various stages of its life cycle. Share your visual in a gallery walk or give a presentation.	Interview a naturalist, animal keeper, trainer, or veterinarian to learn about the types of work they do. If possible, spend a day or half day "shadowing" or assisting the professional. Share your findings. Make a brochure with drawings to illustrate interesting facts about the career you investigated.	Visit a zoo or nature center to study a species of animal in its habitat. Estimate the size and mass of the animals; identify conditions of their habitat such as amount and height of fencing, volume of space, and other physical features. Research the amount of food the animals eat per day and calculate the amount and cost of food per year. Collect data for the various stages in the life cycle of this species. Share your findings.

Figure 31   Outline for a Contract

Name _____

Title of Unit _____

Completion Date _____

Signature of Student _____

Learning Objectives and Key Concepts (Identify what part or parts of the instructional unit students will address in their study)	
Expectations	
Action Plan—including times and tasks	
Resources and Materials	
Assessment—Evidence of Learning	

Figure 32   Contract for a Study of Rocks and Minerals

Name _____

Title of Unit _____**Rocks and Minerals**_____

Completion Date _____

Signature of Student _____

Learning Objectives and Key Concepts	Important Concepts
	Rocks are inorganic natural substances that form large parts of the Earth's crust. Some rocks are made almost entirely of one mineral, but for them to be classified as a mineral, they must be homogeneous, that is, they must have the same chemical composition throughout. Rocks contain more than one mineral.

A **mineral** is a homogeneous inorganic substance having a definite chemical composition. It is usually a solid, but may be a liquid. Most minerals are formed by a combination of several elements, but some are homogeneous physically and chemically if they consist of elements of the same kind throughout.

The **rock cycle** shows the ways that rocks are changed by the processes of weathering, erosion, compaction, cementation, melting, and cooling.

Careers

The science of studying rocks is called **petrology;** a scientist who studies rocks is a **petrologist.**

Scientists who study **mineralogy** (the science of minerals) are **mineralogists.** They observe and define characteristics of minerals and explain their origins and development. Both types of scientists are **geologists** since **geology** studies the origin, composition, and evolution of the earth.

Science-Technology-Society Connections

Minerals and rocks play a vital role in the modern world. Based on current consumption rates, it is estimated that each person in the United States will use more than a million pounds of rocks, minerals, and metals in their lifetime! How, exactly, will you use them?

Identify some of the uses of rocks and minerals in society. |

Figure 32 (Continued)

Expectations	Identify specific objectives this student is expected to achieve. These learning objectives should align with instructional goals from state standards documents. Identify how the students will show learning. Students should keep a notebook of information, activities, and experiences, and summarize learning. Students may communicate learning through projects and products, multimedia presentations or demonstrations, or other novel ways.
Action Plan—including activities and experiments, experiences, direct learning approaches, and timelines	Activities and experiences should be selected from the choice board (see page 110) or designed, but in all cases, they should align with the goals and objectives the student is expected to achieve. Students may choose activities, experiments, projects, community action, model-building, Internet research with PowerPoint presentations, or other approaches based on their interests, learning styles, or intelligences.
Resources and Materials	Materials and resources should be available for students including the following: rock and mineral sets; equipment; chemicals and consumable materials; reference books; computer software programs; approved Internet sites; materials for building models, creating brochures, posters, and other visuals; human resources and organizations; and others, as needed.
Assessment—Evidence of Learning	Students should provide evidence of their learning orally or visually through presentations, demonstrations, or products, as determined when contracts are designed.

Choice Board for Activities

Instructional activities that may be available to students include the following:

- Splish/Splash: How Much H_2O?
  Students will investigate the relationship between the amount of land and water on Earth; students will investigate what makes up the crust of the earth and investigate land masses and oceans on the crust.
- E Is for Earth; E Is for Egg.
  An egg can be used as a model to simulate layers of solid material on the Earth—students will make a model using half an egg and identify the crust and mantle and core. They will draw the cross section and label the drawing.
- A Study of Rocks
  Students will investigate a variety of rocks and identify properties such as color, shape, size, mass, and so forth. One rock can be selected as a "pet rock" and additional information can be learned about that type.
- Layered Rocks
  Students will study sedimentary rocks and observe layers and other properties. A jar of material of various sizes (sand, gravel, silt) can be used to show how layers form.
  Students will find sedimentary rock on a diagram of the Rock Cycle and trace the paths of change that involve sedimentary rock. They will collect data, visualize relationships between sedimentary rock and other rock types, and recognize cause and effect relationships.
- Igneous Rocks
  Students will study igneous rocks and identify properties. They will relate igneous rock to the Rock Cycle and trace the paths of change that involve igneous rock. Students may study crystals and geometric solids as they investigate igneous rock.
- Metamorphic Rocks
  Students will study metamorphic rocks and observe properties unique to this group. They will relate metamorphic rock to the Rock Cycle and trace the paths of change that involve metamorphic rock.
- The Rock Cycle
  Students will use igneous, sedimentary, and metamorphic rocks to make a model of the rock cycle. They will describe the changes that each type of rock can go through over time.

- Volcanic Rocks Revisited: An Introduction to Minerals

    Cookie Analogy—Chocolate chip and nut cookies provide a model "rock" that can be dissected for their component "minerals." Students will observe, classify, and measure quantities; generalize; comprehend and show understanding of minerals as components of rocks.

- Common Minerals

    A number of common minerals can be studied and tested. Students may study mineral sets from their state's Geological Survey. Students may study gemstones and research where they are found, their use, and their economic value. Students might research the properties and common uses of rocks and minerals. Students will find examples of rocks and minerals in their homes, their communities, and their states.

- Careers in Science

    Students can study the careers associated with rocks and minerals. Scientists who studies rocks are *petrologists.* Scientists who study minerals are *mineralogists.* They observe and define characteristics of minerals and explain their origins and development. Both types of scientists are *geologists* since *geology* studies the origin, composition, and evolution of the earth.

- Resources for Learning

    Web sites, videos, and resources for reading about rocks and minerals; community resources, such as museums or collections; clubs; and industrial sites, such as quarries, mines, state geological surveys, and the like.

COMPUTER-BASED TECHNOLOGIES AS TOOLS FOR LEARNING

There has been an explosion of information and communication technologies that offer new and exciting challenges to the teaching and learning of science. Computer-based tools for use in the science classroom include the following:

- Tools for data capturing, processing and interpreting data such as data logging systems, databases, and graphing tools.
- Multimedia software for simulations and virtual labs.
- Publishing and presentation tools.
- Digital recording equipment.
- Computer projection technology.
- Computer-controlled microscopes.

These and other technologies enhance both the practical and theoretical aspects of science teaching and learning. They can expedite and enhance work production and allow more time for thinking, discussion, interpretation, and reflection.

Web sites and commercial software programs provide information for research and extended learning. U.S. government agencies offer a wealth of resources and up-to-date information for teachers and students that address the eight concept categories of science:

- Unifying concepts and processes.
- Science as inquiry.
- Physical science, life science, and earth and space science.
- Science and technology.
- Science in personal and social perspectives.
- History and nature of science.

Following are examples of information that can be obtained from the U.S. government:

- The Environmental Protection Agency (www.EPA.gov) offers information on topics such as acid rain, oil spills, air and water quality, climate change, hazardous waste, and others that relate to the environment.
- The National Aeronautics and Space Administration (www.NASA .gov) provides information, facts, and features for teachers and students about topics such as space flight, space stations, astronauts, activities in space, and so forth.
- The U.S. Geological Survey (www.USGS.gov) provides information to describe and understand the Earth. Maps and information about groundwater, volcanic activity, and earthquakes are just a few of the topics offered at this site.
- The National Oceanic and Atmospheric Administration (www .NOAA.gov) provides a wealth of information about weather including maps, storms, and hazards.
- The U.S. Department of Agriculture (www.USDA.gov) offers valuable information on topics related to food and nutrition, natural resources and the environment, and rural and community development.
- Topics offered by the U.S. Department of Energy (www.energy.gov) include science and technology, energy sources, environment, national security, and health and safety, among others.

The sites not only provide information and resources related to their specific areas, they also provide career information, curriculum guides and activities, and links to sites that offer interactive games for children of all ages. For example, the U.S. Department of Agriculture offers a game for ages 6 to 11 called *My Pyramid Blast Off* (www.mypyramid.gov), which teaches children about food choices and the importance of exercise.

As tools for differentiated learning, computer-based technologies offer students choices and opportunities for active learning. Motivation and engagement result from immediate and visual feedback offered through interactive programs, simulations, and virtual experiments. Computer-based technologies enable students to work collaboratively or independently to conduct research, solve problems, or extend knowledge and work in a variety of settings, including computer labs, classrooms, libraries, or homes.

7 Strategies for Explaining, Applying, and Creating Meaning

During this phase of instruction, students reflect on processes they used and data they collected. They compare their findings with those of other groups and question the validity of results. Through sharing of data and information, discussion of findings and conclusions, and visual displays, students create meaning and deepen their understandings.

The most important aspect of this phase is creating meaning. It is here that students link new learning to prior knowledge to build concept understanding. They create visuals, such as graphs or posters to display learning or use graphic organizers to show relationships between concepts. When they relate and apply concepts to technology and society, they discover the many ways that science impacts their lives.

GROUP DISCUSSION

What is it? Discussion is a technique for sharing processes, data, generalizations, information, ideas, and opinions in an atmosphere where all students feel free to participate.

Why do we use it? Discussion enables students to describe their process and share and assess their learning. Discussion offers a forum for conceptual and procedural knowledge to be shared and clarified and for new information or novel ideas to be introduced.

Good discussion allows teachers to gain insight into student learning as well as to identify errors in process, faulty data or findings, and misconceptions.

What does it look like? Discussion requires a "safe atmosphere" where students can feel comfortable for sharing correct and incorrect responses without "put downs" or criticism. Involving the class in establishing some ground rules for discussion will help students better abide by those rules.

Some rules for discussion might include the following:

- Only one person will speak at a time while others show respect by remaining quiet.
- All participants will do the best they can to provide honest, open, and concise data or information.
- We will critique others as "critical friends" by respecting their views and helping to correct their errors and misunderstandings.
- We will function as a community of learners with a goal of achieving success for all.

Questions for Thinking and Problem Solving

Often, teachers ask questions or pose problems at different levels of Bloom's Taxonomy (Bloom, 1956). See the following, for example:

- Level I, Knowledge-Recall: What did you learn?
- Level II, Comprehension-Understanding: How did you get these data?
- Level III, Application-Transfer: Use this information to predict. . . .
- Level IV, Analysis-Examining: What could you do differently to get more accurate data?
- Level V, Synthesis-Combining: Design an inquiry-based action plan to answer the question.
- Level VI, Evaluation-Rating: How would you rate the solutions that were proposed?

Bloom's levels can also be used to layer the curriculum. Questions and problems posed should be based on the levels of content knowledge and skills appropriate for a group of learners. Once students have acquired basic knowledge and comprehension, new questions can be used to challenge students to think and seek answers at Levels III and beyond. The taxonomy, then, offers diverse ways for students to acquire knowledge or skills in ways that promote learning.

Discussion Starters

Figure 33 shows questions and suggestions for discussion and assignments that allow teachers to provide appropriate thinking for all learners.

Figure 33   Discussion Starters at Six Levels of Thinking

Level I: Knowledge

1. What are the properties of these objects?
2. What are the stages in the life cycle of the butterfly?
3. What are the principles of cell theory?
4. Who was Albert Einstein?
5. What is the source of energy for food chains?
6. Arrange these historical events in a sequence.
7. What is one use for the Periodic Table?

Level II: Comprehension

1. Which of the following represents the best definition of a theory?
2. What does the graph show us about __?
3. Explain forces that drive the rock cycle.
4. Which drawing shows the relationship between force and motion?
5. The data show the change in height of the plant in a week. What will the height be in two weeks?

Level III: Application

1. Find examples of Newton's Laws of Motion in the school or on the school site.
2. How will the disappearance of one component of a food chain affect the others?
3. What time of day is a sunbather most likely to be sunburned and why?
4. How can you use a mirror to identify bilateral symmetry?
5. How can your class reduce the amount of paper they use in a week?

Level IV: Analysis

1. Examine the two pictures. Explain how the landscape changed over time and suggest reasons for the change.
2. What does the graph tell us about the relationship between X and Y?
3. Based on your data, what conclusion can you draw?
4. Explain why one habitat is more suitable than another for an animal.

Level V: Synthesis

1. Design an experiment to test a hypothesis.
2. Create a book with words and pictures to teach Newton's Laws to another person.
3. Create a Rube Goldberg-type contraption using five or more simple machines to solve a problem.
4. Invent something to simplify a task.

Level VI: Evaluation

1. What were the strengths and weaknesses of your experimental design?
2. Use the set of criteria to rate the different types of microscopes.
3. Identify the fallacies in the argument.
4. Identify and discuss the economic and social trade-offs to a solution to a problem.
5. Which of the products would be the best choice for a given situation? Provide data to support your choice.

NONLINGUISTIC REPRESENTATIONS
FOR K–8 SCIENCE

What are they? According to the dual-coding theory of information storage, knowledge is stored in two forms: linguistic and imagery. The imagery mode of information storage is referred to as nonlinguistic representation. These representations are also called graphic organizers as they are used to organize information into meaningful schemes that are stored as mental images in the brain.

Why do we use them? Marzano, Pickering, and Pollack (2001, p. 73) reported that "explicitly engaging students in the creation of nonlinguistic representations stimulates and increases activity in the brain." Nonlinguistic representations elaborate on knowledge and require students to explain their models and the thinking that created the models.

Research prepared by the Institute for the Advancement of Research in Education (2003) identified 29 scientifically based research studies that support the use of graphic organizers for improving student learning and performance across grade levels with diverse students in a range of content areas including science, social studies, and mathematics. They were found to be effective in improving reading comprehension and enhancing thinking and learning skills, such as organizing ideas and categorizing concepts.

What do they look like? Physical and human models, charts, data tables and graphs, graphic organizers, pictures and pictographs are all types of nonlinguistic representations that describe or explain phenomena. Nonlinguistic representations are valuable tools for learning in that they provide mental models for retaining and recalling information.

Charts

Charts can be designed by teachers or students to accommodate data from one day to one month. For example, students might use a chart to record results of an experiment for one class period, weather conditions for a week, or phases of the moon for a month. Charts should be designed with space to write descriptions, record numerical data, and draw pictures, as appropriate. Figures 34 and 35 show two different types of charts.

Data Tables and Graphs

Data tables and graphs are commonly used in inquiry-based science since data collecting is a key component of inquiry. They may not be of significance in differentiating instruction except to note that data collection

Figure 34   Weekly Weather Chart

Week of _____ Time:	Sky Conditions	Temperature	Precipitation	Wind Speed and Direction	Other Observations
Monday					
Tuesday					
Wednesday					
Thursday					
Friday					

Figure 35   Layers of the Earth

Layer	Description of Features	Temperature Range	Other Information
Lithosphere	Solid rock, mostly basalt and granite. Oceanic crust = "young rock"; about 6 km thick. 1% of Earth. Continental crust = 25–90 km; older rock.	Between -127°F to 136°F (-88°C to 58°C)	Coldest recorded temperature = Vostok on the continent of Antarctica in July 1983. Hottest recorded temperature = Libya on the continent of Africa in September 1922
Mantle	Made up of hot, dense, semisolid rock made of silicon, oxygen, magnesium, and iron; 3000 km thick.	Approximately 1110°C to 3,000°C	It is the largest layer of the Earth, 1800 miles thick. The movement of the mantle is the reason that the plates of the Earth move! They "float" on it like oil floats on water.
Core	Outer core, 2200 km; mostly molten iron. Inner core 1250 km; mostly solid iron with some nickel and cobalt.	Outer to inner core: 3000° C to 5000°C	Temperatures based on theoretical models.

and display should be part of every investigation that students do whether it be for all-group, small group, or individual instruction. Graphs provide a visual representation of data that makes data more meaningful and memorable for visual learners.

It is important to emphasize the need to have well designed and labeled tables on which to record data in the form of words, pictures, or numbers prior to creating graphs as visual displays for data. Data tables may be designed by teachers or students and may be enhanced by providing space for written descriptions or recording "other" information. Figures 36, 37, and 38 show various types of data tables.

Figure 36 Data Table for Properties of Objects at the Primary Level

Object	Rough or Smooth	Color	Length	Mass	Magnetic Yes or No	Other

Figure 37 Data Table for Magnetic Attraction at the Early Intermediate Level

Prediction: Will Magnets Attract? Yes or No	Arrangement of Magnets	Observation: Did Magnets Attract? Yes or No
	[S N] [S N]	
	[S N] [N S]	
	[N S] [N S]	
	[N S] [S N]	

Figure 38 Data Table for Comparing Bounce Height of Hot and Cold Balls at Middle Grades

Trial No.	Hot Ball Bounce Height	Cold Ball Bounce Height
1	cm	cm
2	cm	cm
3	cm	cm
4	cm	cm

SOURCE: Modified from Gartrell and Schafer (1990)

Figure 39   Data Table and Graph for Calorie Count for Common Food

Type of Food	No. of Calories
Bread—cracked wheat—1 slice	60
Apple—medium	80
Milk—8 oz	100
Hamburger, lean, broiled—4 oz	230
Chocolate bar	240
Salami—4 oz	350

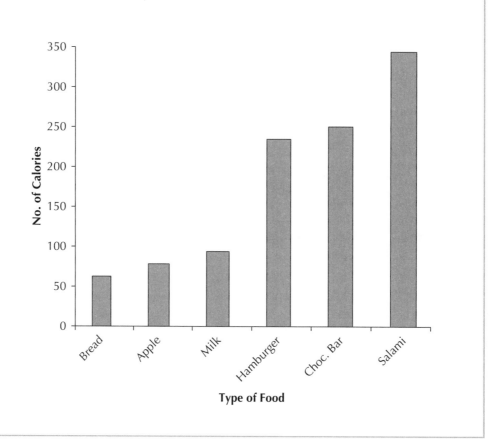

Creating Graphs

Once data have been collected, there are opportunities for students to create graphs to visually display those data.

Rules for graphing

a. Graphs should have a title.

b. Each axis should be carefully considered and labeled with variable or units.
   With experimental data:

- Horizontal axis: manipulated variable (independent).
- Vertical axis: responding variable (dependent).

c. Select a reasonable scale for each axis. Consider data and what you want to show. Increments should be evenly spaced on each axis. The data need not start at zero.
   Types of graphs:

- Bar graphs.
- Histograms (shows frequency of occurrence).
- Pictographs.
- Line graphs (often used to show change over time or continuous flow).

Bar Graphs

Figure 39 shows a bar graph, Figure 40 shows a histogram, and Figure 41 shows a pictograph with data sets.

A pictograph is a special type of bar graph in which a symbol is used to represent a number.

Line Graphs

Line graphs show a relationship between two variables. Figure 42 shows a line graph.

Circle Graphs

A circle is used to represent 100% of something. Parts of a circle are shaded to show parts or percentage of the whole. Figure 43 shows a circle graph.

Figure 40 Data Table and Histogram for Eye Color in a Class

Eye Color	Number
Blue	4
Brown	7
Green	2
Gray	1
Hazel	1
Other	0

Number of Students	Blue	Brown	Green	Gray	Hazel	Other
		X				
		X				
		X				
	X	X				
	X	X				
	X	X	X			
	X	X	X	X	X	

Eye Color

Figure 41 Pictograph

A pictograph is a special type of bar graph in which a symbol is used to represent a number.

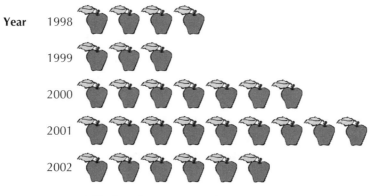

KEY: 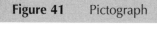 = 100 bushels of apples

Yield of Apples From the Friendly Farmer Orchard

Figure 42 Data and Graph Showing Expectations of Life (in years) in the United States for Men and Women

Year	Men	Women
1909	50	53
1919	56	58
1929	59	62
1939	63	67
1949	66	72
1959	67.5	74
1969	68	75

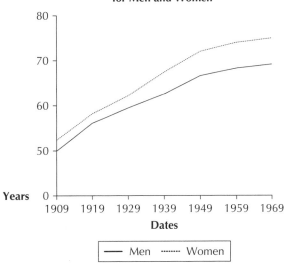

Expectation of Life in the United States for Men and Women

——— Men ·········· Women

Figure 43 A Circle Graph

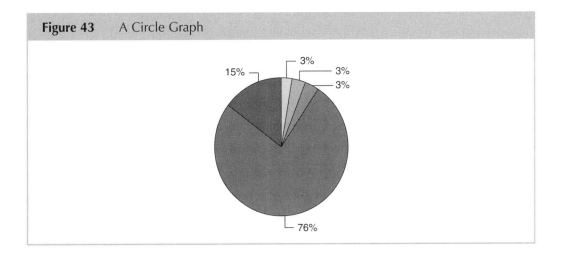

SIX TYPES OF GRAPHIC ORGANIZERS

What are they? Graphic organizers are common nonlinguistic representations that challenge students to think about relationships that exist between concepts and organize information in systematic ways.

Why are they used? Students may create graphic organizers to show the ways they frame thought, link new learning to prior learning, or make connections to their lives, to technology, and to society.

What do they look like? There are at least six ways of organizing knowledge and an assortment of variations. Basic organizers are tools for helping students to understand the various types of relationships that exist between concepts. Organizers that are described in this chapter are as follows:

- **Descriptive:** A main idea at the center with subcategories or properties radiating from the center; often includes "linking words" to identify relationship.
- **Sequential:** Used to show a logical sequence of events, such as a flow chart or timeline.
- **Process causal:** Used to show a sequence of causal events or cause and effect relationships.
- **Categorical:** A horizontal or vertical tree-like configuration used for classification.
- **Comparison or relational**: Identifies similarities and differences or comparisons between two or more objects, events, and so forth.
- **Problem or solution**: Used to show thinking about a problem by identifying plausible solutions.

Figures 44 to 49 show examples of the six relationships using concepts or events from elementary science.

Figure 44   Descriptive

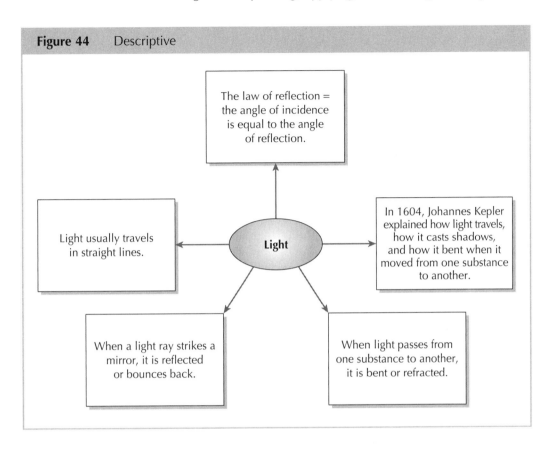

Figure 45   Sequence or Timeline

1981	1983	1986	1988	1994
First U.S. Space Shuttle Launched (John Young and Robert Crippen)	Dr. Sally Ride: First Woman in Space; mission specialist on STS-7, launched from Kennedy Space Center, Florida, on June 18, 1983	Challenger explosion kills seven astronauts and one teacher	Discovery becomes first shuttle after Challenger	Scientists find black hole using Hubble Telescope

Significant Events in the History of Space

Figure 46   Process Causal or Cause and Effect

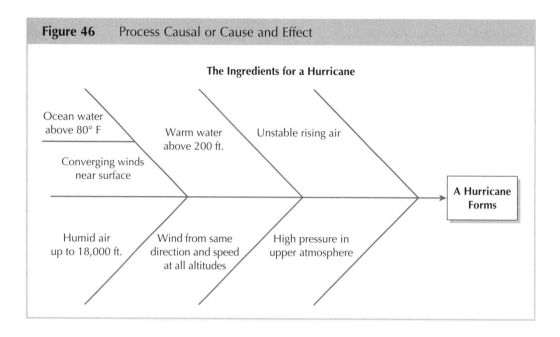

Figure 47   Concept Categories

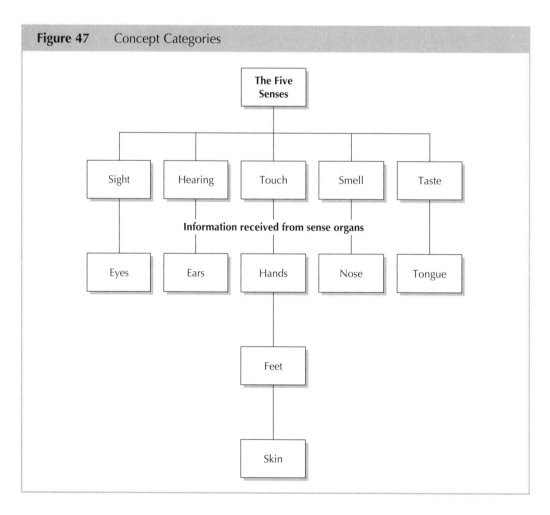

Figure 48   Comparison or Relational

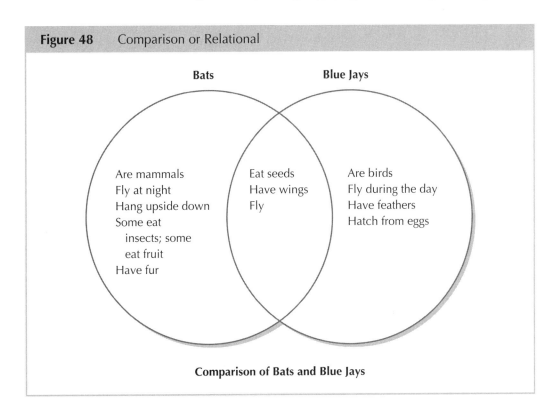

Comparison of Bats and Blue Jays

Figure 49   Problem or Solution

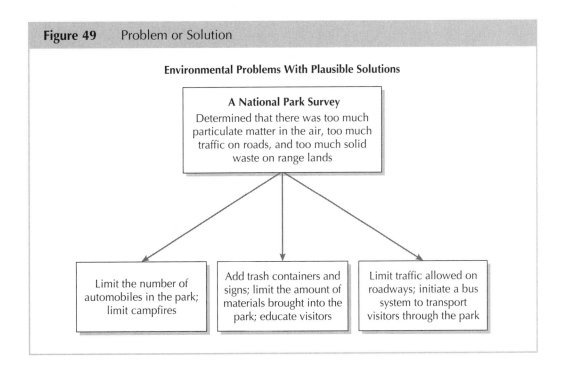

FOUR-CORNER ORGANIZER

What is it? A four-corner organizer is a type of graphic organizer that provides comparative information about four organisms, objects, or events.

Why do we use it? The graphic provides a visual display of data that can be easily compared to note similarities and differences.

What does it look like? An example of a four-corner organizer is used to compare the life cycles of animals from different groups (see Figure 50). Here, students have selected four animal groups to study—mammal, reptile, amphibian, and insect.

A FOUR-CORNER ORGANIZER FOR COMPARING LIFE CYCLES OF ANIMALS

For this inquiry-based activity, primary or intermediate level students are divided into four groups with each group studying one of four animal groups. They begin by generating inquiry questions they have about the life cycle of their animal group and develop an action plan for learning about it.

Action plans are developed by each group of students with assistance from the teacher. For example, students studying mammals might visit a zoo or breeding farm or invite a dog breeder to come to their class; students studying insects might study the changes from mealworms to beetles or manage and observe a butterfly garden; students studying reptiles may visit a zoo or pet store or invite a biologist to learn about life cycles of turtles; students studying amphibians might manage an aquarium with tadpoles and observe their changes.

A four-corner organizer is used to show characteristics of each of the four animal groups. One animal from each group is selected for the graphic. The organizer shows the stages in the life cycle, the ways the animal changes as it goes through its life cycle, and the behaviors that the animal inherits from its parents. Students present their findings to the group and each student records the organizer in a notebook.

National Geographic has theme sets of beautifully illustrated books on specific topics, including animal life cycles. The animals included in the life cycle theme books are the giant panda (mammal), the Komodo dragon (reptile), the poison dart frog (amphibian), and the monarch butterfly (insect). Three key concepts are presented in each book: the stages in the life cycle of the animal, the ways the animals change as they go through their life cycle, and the difference between inherited behaviors passed to the animal from its parents and learned behaviors that the animal acquires throughout its life. In addition, the books include pictures and illustrations, provide opportunities for students to reflect on important concepts, and offer interesting stories about the animals.

Figure 50 shows a four-corner organizer that compares the life cycles of the monarch butterfly, the poison dart frog, the Komodo dragon, and the giant panda. The center of the organizer shows the four major animal groups. The specific animal from each group is named and information is provided about its habitat, its physical features and distinguishing characteristics, the number and names of life cycle stages, and its inherited behaviors. The graphic enables students to observe similarities and differences at a glance.

Figure 50   Four-Corner Organizer for Life Cycles of Animals

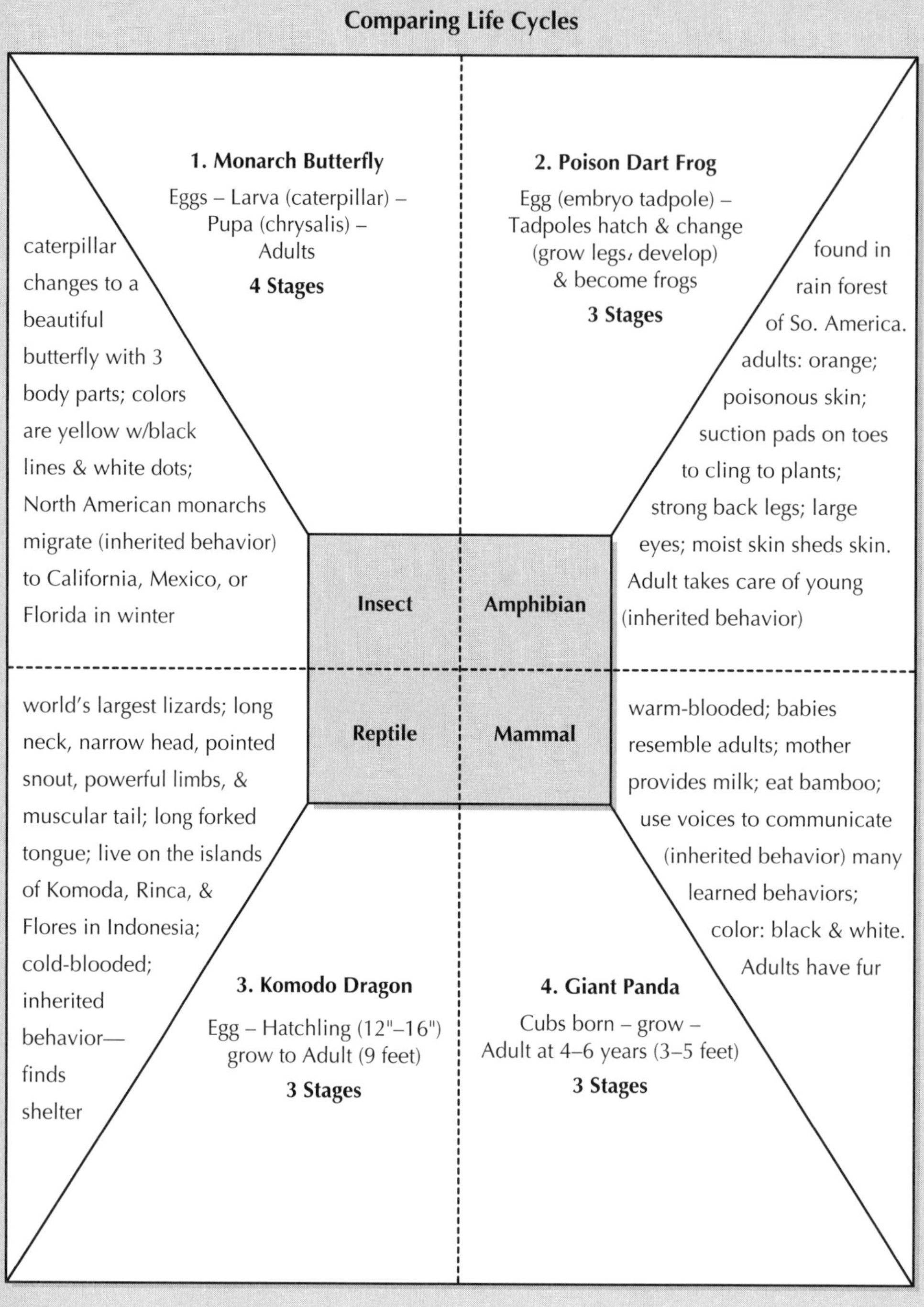

Comparing Life Cycles

1. Monarch Butterfly

Eggs – Larva (caterpillar) –
Pupa (chrysalis) –
Adults

4 Stages

caterpillar changes to a beautiful butterfly with 3 body parts; colors are yellow w/black lines & white dots; North American monarchs migrate (inherited behavior) to California, Mexico, or Florida in winter

2. Poison Dart Frog

Egg (embryo tadpole) –
Tadpoles hatch & change
(grow legs, develop)
& become frogs

3 Stages

found in rain forest of So. America. adults: orange; poisonous skin; suction pads on toes to cling to plants; strong back legs; large eyes; moist skin sheds skin. Adult takes care of young (inherited behavior)

Insect   **Amphibian**

Reptile   **Mammal**

world's largest lizards; long neck, narrow head, pointed snout, powerful limbs, & muscular tail; long forked tongue; live on the islands of Komoda, Rinca, & Flores in Indonesia; cold-blooded; inherited behavior— finds shelter

warm-blooded; babies resemble adults; mother provides milk; eat bamboo; use voices to communicate (inherited behavior) many learned behaviors; color: black & white. Adults have fur

3. Komodo Dragon

Egg – Hatchling (12"–16")
grow to Adult (9 feet)

3 Stages

4. Giant Panda

Cubs born – grow –
Adult at 4–6 years (3–5 feet)

3 Stages

8 Strategies for Elaborating and Extending Learning

New questions will arise as students investigate key concepts. Opportunities for extended learning enable students to go beyond the basic concepts and skills around which a unit of instruction is structured. Through extended learning students can increase their breadth of knowledge by making applications to technology and society, their personal lives, community problems and issues, and careers in science.

BEYOND THE BASICS

Students should be encouraged to ask new questions about the topics they investigate. They may design new investigations where they collect data, formulate conclusions, and communicate findings. Or they may prefer to research topics related to the history and nature of science or science phenomena or careers in a specific area of science.

Besides printed materials, such as reference books, trade books, posters, brochures, and other printed materials, students can extend learning through the use of computers and audio and video equipment. Videotapes, audio presentations, software programs, and reliable Web sites offer a wealth of information to students who wish to extend their learning.

Problem-based learning, involvement in competitions such as Science Olympiad (www.soinc.org), visits to informal science centers, action research, and community service projects also extend learning and help students develop deeper understandings of the relationships between science, technology, and society.

Many of the strategies for acquiring and exploring are also applicable to elaborating and extending learning (see Chapter 6).

GAMES THAT ENHANCE LEARNING

What are they? Serious games are those that are focused on learning specific concepts or skills that are part of the curriculum. Games are a novel way to introduce and define concepts, but also provide an interesting and novel way to reinforce and apply concepts and practice skills. Some games offer problems that require strategic thinking and reasoning to solve. Games range from those involving an entire class of students to those designed for small groups or individuals.

Why do we use them? Games allow students to generate, reinforce, use, or apply concepts and practice skills individually or with a group. Games are often engaging and motivating and can be used to show practical applications of concepts.

What do they look like? There are many types of educational games ranging from traditional board games (Scrabble) and "game show" games (Jeopardy) to games involving physical activity and role-playing (predator and prey) to computer-based games. Care should be taken to select games that relate directly to important concepts and skills and include various levels of thinking to challenge students.

Cubing

What is it? Cubing is a strategy that uses the six sides on a cube to help students think or process information at different levels.

Why do we use it? Since cubing is a technique for considering topics or issues from six different levels of thought, it works well to expand one's perspective when locked into a particular way of thinking (Cowan & Cowan, 1980; Tomlinson, 2001).

Cubing offers a chance to differentiate learning by readiness (familiarity with content or level of skill), student interest, or learning profile (multiple intelligences). Cubes may vary in color and tasks depending on the abilities and interests of students. They add an element of novelty and fun to learning by providing uniqueness to the lesson. It is a great strategy for tactile or kinesthetic learners as it reinforces concept understanding or extends or demonstrates learning in new ways.

What does it look like? Think of a cube or die. Each of the six sides of the cube will have a different "way of thinking" on it. See the following, for example:

- Describe it
- Compare it
- Associate it
- Analyze it
- Apply it
- Argue for or against it

The commands on cubes will vary with tasks and should be appropriate for the content and level of readiness of the group. Cubes may also be constructed with tasks in a particular area of the multiple intelligences such as verbal or linguistic, logical or mathematical, spatial, or naturalistic. Students can also make up cubes and trade them to review content, concepts, and skills.

Cubing With Questions About the Moon

Cubes might have prompts from each level of Bloom's Taxonomy or perhaps one of the multiple intelligences. The following example (Figure 51) is one that can be used to review knowledge or to challenge thinking about the moon. Figure 51 shows the six sides of a cube with questions about the earth's moon.

Jigsaw

What is it? A jigsaw strategy is one way of increasing interdependence among students, as well as a way of increasing individual accountability. Jigsaw (Aronson, 1978; Slavin, 1994) is a very effective strategy but not one that would be used with students until they have the social skills to deal with several members in a group as well as the skills to work independently.

Why do we use it? Jigsaw is a powerful strategy for covering more material in less time and for extending learning. It enhances learning and increases retention. The jigsaw strategy facilitates the sharing of responsibility for learning. It helps focus energy in a task and provides structure for the learning. This strategy has interpersonal and intrapersonal components that also allow students to process information and move and interact with a variety of class members to gain a greater perspective on the

Figure 51   Six Questions About the Earth's Moon

	1. Describe the features of the moon and explain why it looks different at different times throughout the month.	
2. Compare it: Trace the history of telescopes and their use in identifying features of the moon. How has knowledge of the moon changed over time?	3. Associate: Consider features of the moon. How is it similar to and different from other objects in the solar system?	4. Apply: Use a visual or make a drawing and explain the reflection of sunlight from the moon to the earth at various times of the month.
	5. Analyze: Consider the conditions on the moon. What would a human need to survive there?	
	6. Argue for or against the following: Should NASA continue to explore ways for humans to live on the moon?	

knowledge or skills that are targeted for learning. In addition, it offers many chances for elaborative rehearsal and use of higher order thinking through dialogue.

What does it look like? Students begin in a base or home group of three or four and are given letters, numbers, or names that will help them form "expert groups." In the expert group, students are to access information or learn new material or skills that they will, in turn, teach to their base group. When they return to the base group, they teach their group members what they have learned.

Figure 52   Jigsaw

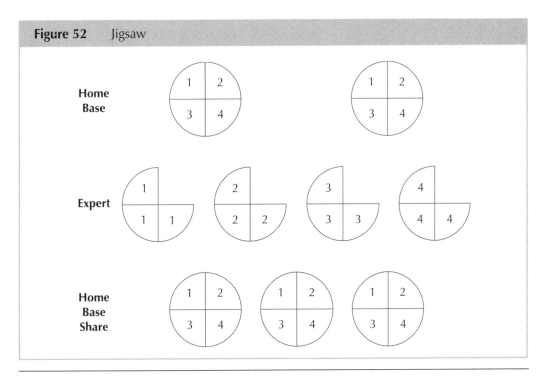

SOURCE: Gregory & Chapman (2007). *Differentiated Instructional Strategies: One Size Doesn't Fit All,* 2nd ed. Thousand Oaks, CA: Corwin Press. Used With Permission.

JIGSAW FOR AN INTERMEDIATE UNIT ON PLANTS

Following a study of plants, groups of four students might be given information about four different aspects of a plant that is an important part of their diet, such as the potato. Each person in the group will read and discuss one of the four topics in an "expert group"— one person from each of the other groups, and report back to their "home group" for sharing interesting facts and information.

The potato may be studied from a variety of perspectives, including the following:

- The potato as a plant, which describes such things as the characteristics of the plant, the potato as a tuber, ideal conditions for growth, and potato "eyes" as buds for new growth.
- The history of potatoes, which tells of their origin in South America, their discovery by Spanish conquistadors in search of gold and silver in the late 1400s and early 1500s, their introduction

to Ireland in the mid-1700s, and the devastating Irish Potato Famine in the 1800s.

- The nutritional value of potatoes as an excellent source of vitamin C, potassium, calcium, and fiber.
- The contributions of American horticulturist Luther Burbank, who developed a new and improved variety of potato, the Russet Burbank, in the late 1800s, which has gone through a few genetic changes, but is still very popular today.

Individual accountability is built into the process by having each member turn in a report, a test, or quiz on the material learned or by calling on students randomly to report for their group.

Jigsaws can be differentiated for students by giving them different materials and content to match different levels of readiness. Products, projects, or other authentic tasks and assessments that are expected from the group, based on their preferences and multiple intelligences, offer other ways to differentiate.

ANALOGIES AND SIMILES

Analogies

Analogical thought can be developed through K–8 science. Questions and discussions that focus on similarities and differences in structures of organisms, cause and effect relationships in events, structures and functions in living and nonliving things, and relationships of persons to places take students to a level of thinking that enables them to create analogies.

Analogical thought has two basic components (Hofstadter, 1995):

- The process of situation-perception.
- The process of mapping.

Analogies are created from perceptions of aspects of the structures of two situations which, in some sense, are identical.

Some of the types of situations on which analogies in science might be based are shown in the left column of Figure 53. The column on the right shows examples of analogies for each type of situation.

Similes

A simile is a comparison of two unlike things, using "like" or "as" in the comparison. Similes are considered by some to be a type of metaphor.

Figure 53   Types of Analogies and Examples in Science

Type of Situations	Analogies in Science
Part to Whole	Wing: Bird, Arm: Human
Cause and Effect	Spicy Food: Indigestion, Dust, Sneeze
Time	Prophase: Mitosis, Starting Line: Race
Gender	Stallion: Mare, Boy: Girl
Antonyms	Hot: Cold, Left: Right
Group and Member	Bird: Duck, Reptile: Turtle
Symbol	Smokey the Bear: Fire Safety, Red Light: Stop
Creation or Creator	Painting: Artist, Vaccine: Scientist
Age	Kitten: Cat, Tadpole: Frog
Function to Object	See: Eye, Hear: Ear
Person to Place	Curator: Museum, Scientist: Laboratory
Object to Tool	Planet: Telescope, Slide: Microscope
Synonyms	Observe: Taste, Write: Record

SOURCE: *Eight Essentials of Inquiry-Based Science* (Hammerman, 2006c).

Similes for a Middle Grade Unit on Cells

As a follow-up to a study of cells, students can create similes by comparing a cell to a large system and describing how parts of a cell function in similar ways to parts of the system. The comparison requires that students have knowledge of both the structures and functions of cell parts and the structures and functions of components of the system to which the cell will be compared (see Figure 54).

Students research and identify the major components of a system of their choice and describe ways that the components of the system function similarly to organelles in the cell. A graphic organizer may be used to show the system and its relationship to a cell. Students may compare a cell to a school, a candy factory, a city, a manufacturing plant, an automobile, or other complex system.

Figure 54 Simile for Cells

The cell is like a city:

  a. The **nucleus** is like **city hall** because it regulates all of the activities in the cell.

  b. The **cell wall** is like a **stone wall** around a medieval city because it is rigid, surrounds the cell, and provides support and protection.

  c. **Chloroplasts** are like the **power plants** because they enable plants to harvest energy from sunlight to make glucose and oxygen, $C_6H_{12}O_6 + 6O_2$ from carbon dioxide and water.

  d. Others are as follows: cytoplasm, ribosomes, Golgi Apparatus, vacuoles, mitochondria, and so forth.

Challenge Question: Identify one or more ways that the cell is different from the system you have selected.

9 Strategies for Assessing and Evaluating Learning

ASSESSMENT AND EVALUATION

What is it? As a general term, *assessment* encompasses all activities that provide feedback to teachers and students about learning. When evidence of learning is sought for the purpose of modifying instruction to accommodate the needs, interests, and abilities of students, it is called *formative assessment.*

Evaluation is the comparison of a performance to a standard. Evaluation generally compares what students know and are able to do following instruction to a set of goals and standards. This is often done through standardized tests or teacher-made tests that are administered after instruction has occurred. Such assessments are *summative* in nature. Generally, summative assessments are converted to symbols or grades for communicating how well a student performed relative to a set of standards-based learning objectives using a system designed and understood by school district administrators, teachers, and parents.

Why do we use it? Teachers need to be accountable for student learning. Assessments provide the tools for measuring student progress toward reaching instructional goals and standards. The feedback offered through assessments provides data that are valuable for both monitoring student progress and for guiding instruction to accommodate student needs, interests, and abilities.

Through an extensive survey of research related to formative assessment, Black and Wiliam (1998) concluded that strengthening the practice of formative assessment produces significant and often substantial learning gains. The researchers also found evidence that improved formative assessment reduced the range of achievement by helping low performing students, while raising achievement overall.

Implications for differentiating instruction: Feedback about learning informs teachers as to whether students are at the novice or beginning level, a practitioner level approaching mastery, or an advanced or mastery level. Teachers can then guide novice learners to relearning activities, direct instruction, or tutoring, practitioners to additional investigations to reinforce concepts, and advanced level students to extended learning or problem-based learning.

What does it look like? Formative assessment is a continuous flow of information about student achievement. Assessments based on important concepts and skills define the desired goals, provide evidence of student learning, and enable teachers to adjust assignments for further learning.

ASSESSMENT STRATEGIES IN THE SCIENCE CLASSROOM

Figure 55 identifies an array of tools and strategies that may be used to gather evidence of student learning for both formative and summative assessment. Suggestions are given for the types of learning that might be best assessed with each tool, and examples are offered for the science classroom. Assessments should be carefully designed to align with important learning goals and standards and provide useful data about what students know and are able to do.

PERFORMANCE TASKS FOR LEARNING AND ASSESSMENT

Clearly, if we want to assess thinking and problem solving along with other valued content understandings, skills, and dispositions, we must provide opportunities for students to show, in a variety of ways, what they know and are able to do. Performance tasks are linked to important learning goals and standards and provide a means for monitoring student growth and learning over time.

Performance tasks may be designed to assess student knowledge and skills and administered apart from instruction, as with a paper-and-pencil task or a lab practical. Or performance tasks may be embedded in instruction so that students are learning or reinforcing new concepts and skills while demonstrating knowledge or ability related to learning objectives.

Figure 55 Assessment in the Science Classroom

Type of Assessment	What It Assesses	What It Looks Like in the Science Classroom
Observation Checklists (A list of desirable behaviors that students exhibit over time)	• Dispositions • Behaviors • Ways of thinking, acting, and interacting • Progress or task completion	• Student works well in a cooperative learning group • Student shows respect for living things and science equipment • Student exhibits honesty, persistence, thinking, and motivation • Student shares ideas and helps colleagues • Student shows progress in completing tasks
Interviews and Dialog (Formal or informal conversations between teacher and student throughout the learning process)	• Understanding of directions • Use of appropriate procedures • Accuracy of observations or data • New questions	• Student is "on task" • Student gives clarification of data or written work • Student demonstrates concept understanding • Student asks new, relevant questions for further inquiry
Learning Log or Notebooks (Written and pictorial records of student work: thinking and processing, action plans, research information and data, conclusion, connections, extensions, and so forth)	• Rationale and thinking • Written descriptions of background information, action plans, observations, procedures, data, graphs, conclusions, summaries, and other components of investigations • Visuals that show thinking and meaning • Meaning and links to prior knowledge	• Students record inquiry questions, problems, and hypotheses • Students describe prior knowledge and predictions • Students show action plans and describe processes used in investigations • Data tables, graphs, charts, and graphic organizers are completed and accurate • Pictures, diagrams, and illustrations show concept understanding • Conclusions and summaries are accurate • Students identify links to self, technology, and prior knowledge • Students describe next steps and show new questions

Teacher-Made Tests (Force choice or open response questions that enable students to show knowledge or understanding of important concepts and skills)	• Vocabulary and concept understanding
	• Relationships between concepts
	• Knowledge or understanding of skills
		• Students will show understanding of concepts, skills, and thinking through the following:
		  o Forced choice and open response questions
		  o Interpretations of graphs, drawings, or visuals

(Continued)

Figure 55 (Continued)

Type of Assessment	What It Assesses	What It Looks Like in the Science Classroom
		• Data analyses • Concept applications • Written explanations of solutions to problems
Products and Projects (A multidimensional approach to learning often involving the design and building of something new; a novel or alternative approach to learning involving research or problem solving)	• Ability to access and use new information purposefully • Ability to design or develop a product that relates to a key concept • Show creativity and ability to make applications • Problem-solving skills	• Students create brochures or posters or other visuals requiring them to access and use new information • Students write reports based on research • Students create products such as models, mobiles, or dioramas that apply concepts • Students solve problems using technological designs
Performance Tasks (Paper-and-pencil tasks and hands-on activities that require students to apply or demonstrate learning)	• Ability to apply learning to new problem • Understanding of concepts • Use of process and thinking skills • Logical reasoning	• Students apply concepts and skills through drawings and descriptions to new problems • Students demonstrate understanding of concepts and skills in a variety of ways
Portfolios (Collections of student work over time; work provides evidence of levels of concept understanding, skills, dispositions, and thinking)	• Shows concept understanding and skill development • Work samples gathered over time show change in thinking and ability to solve problems	• Notebook entries, lab reports, and summaries show concept understanding, development of skills, and thinking and reasoning • Student is able to apply concepts through inventions, projects, and products • Work shows scientific thinking and problem solving
Criterion Referenced Tests (Questions aligned with instructional objectives; include multiple questions on a single concept)	• Determine levels of understanding of concepts and skills related to the district or school curriculum	• Students show concept understanding through teacher-made tests designed around taught curriculum • Students score well on benchmark tests based on state or district curriculum
Norm Referenced Tests (High stakes tests; questions related to state or national goals and standards)	• Standards-based concepts and principles • Thinking and process skills	• Student scores on commercially produced tests (Basic Skills; Advanced Placement; International Baccalaureate; NAEP; SAT; ACT) • Student scores on state tests

Performance tasks that are embedded in instruction do the following:

- Use engaging contexts through which evidence of student learning might be assessed.
- Offer problems to solve or products to complete.
- Identify authentic indicators of learning that show knowledge and understanding of the following:
  o Concepts of life, earth and space, and physical science.
  o Skills.
  o Valued dispositions.
  o The history and nature of science.
  o Science as inquiry.
  o The relationship of science and technology.
  o Science in personal and social perspectives.
  o Assessment indicators of learning through a rubric.

Performance tasks require students to personalize their understanding about important concepts. Students may create a graphic organizer, a brochure, poster, project, or model, show a solution to a problem, design and conduct an experiment, or write summaries of learning through letters or reports.

PRIMARY LEVEL PERFORMANCE ASSESSMENT: MAKING HEALTHY CHOICES

Standards: Science in Personal and Social Perspectives—Personal Health

Key concepts: Good nutrition is essential to good health. It is important to make wise choices for meals and snacks to obtain the nutrients needed to stay healthy.

Students should be able to apply recommendations from the U.S. Department of Agriculture (USDA) Food Guide Pyramid to show their understanding of a balanced meal. Students will explain their choices and how the meals meet the standards for "good health."

Prior experience: This task will be used as part of a summative assessment for a unit on nutrition. This performance assumes that students are familiar with the following:

- The USDA Food Guide Pyramid (http://www.mypyramid .gov/kids/index.html).
- Foods from each category on the USDA Food Guide Pyramid.

(Continued)

(Continued)

- The recommended servings for children their age.
- Analyzing nutritional values of foods, meals, and snacks.
- Sorting and classifying pictures of foods into categories from the USDA Food Guide Pyramid.
- The *MyPyramid Blast Off Game*—An interactive computer game where kids can reach Planet Power by fueling their rocket with food and physical activity. "Fuel" tanks for each food group help students keep track of how their choices fit into the USDA Food Guide Pyramid. It is designed for children ages 6–11 (http://www.mypyramid.gov/kids/index.html).
- Analyzing personal eating habits.
- Making recommendations for diet and exercise for good health.

Rationale: The task will allow students to apply the recommendations from the Food Guide Pyramid for an eight-year-old child of average height and weight who gets approximately 30 to 60 minutes of exercise per day and show their understanding of a "balanced meal" by designing and drawing a healthy lunch that includes all food groups (grains, vegetables, fruits, milk, and meat or beans). They will write or explain their choices and tell why their sample meal is "healthy."

Materials per person: Needed are idea and drawing pages to illustrate "Making Healthy Choices" (see the sample on page 148); a copy of the scoring rubric for the task (optional).

Presenting the task: Create a context for the assessment task by telling students they have received a letter from the principal asking for their help in suggesting healthy lunches that might be served in the school cafeteria. They have been asked to use information from the Food Guide Pyramid, make choices, and to draw a "healthy lunch" for students their age. They are also asked to provide an explanation for their choices so that the principal and others will know why the lunch is healthy and appropriate for their age group. The suggestions will be shared with the principal and cafeteria staff.

Performance task: Give each student a chart of recommendations from the Food Guide Pyramid for students their age and an empty plate data page. Review with the students the Food Guide Pyramid food groups and the recommendations for an eight-year-old child of average height and weight who gets approximately 30 to 60 minutes of exercise per day, directions for the task, and the scoring rubric before they individually complete the task.

On the "Ideas Page," students should make a list of at least three foods from each category they might want to include in the meal and record them on the chart. They should select items from their list and draw their sample meal on the empty plate and label each item on the plate. They should write an explanation for their choices or verbally explain the reasons for their choices and the ways the meal matches the recommendations from the Food Guide Pyramid.

Directions for Students

Review the information from the Food Guide Pyramid for recommended servings for your grade level and what you have learned in this nutrition unit to design a healthy lunch for students your age.

1. Review the food groups and the recommendations on the Food Guide Pyramid.

2. Make a list of at least three items from each food group that could be included in the lunch (you do not have to include all of them in the final meal).

3. Select items from your list and draw a healthy meal (on the empty plate data sheet) for a child your age that includes something from each of the food groups.

4. Label each item in the meal.

5. Write (or be ready to explain) the reasons for your choices and how your meal matches the recommendations from the Food Guide Pyramid.

SCORING RUBRIC FOR MAKING HEALTHY CHOICES

A generalized rubric is shown in Figure 56 for the task that aligns with the objectives of the unit. The task might be designed to address other learning goals, such as a student's ability to write complete sentences, properly spell words, or show subject and verb agreement. Four levels of achievement are shown for the task; levels and descriptions may be adjusted to more appropriately match student ability levels.

(Continued)

(Continued)

Name: _____ Date: _____

Idea Page for Making Healthy Choices

Recommendations From the Food Guide Pyramid

The recommended food pattern for an eight-year-old child of average height and weight who gets approximately 30 to 60 minutes of exercise per day

Food Group	Amount per Day	Possible Foods to Include in a Healthy Meal
Grains	5 ounces	
Vegetables	2 cups	
Fruits	1 ½ cups	
Milk	2 cups	
Meat and Beans	5 ounces	

Name_____ Date_____

Drawing of Healthy Lunch

Why My Lunch Is Healthy

Figure 56   Scoring Rubric for Making Healthy Choices

Indicator of Learning	Novice	Apprentice	Practitioner	Expert
Listed foods from each category on the Food Guide	List is incomplete or shows little match to guide	Examples are weak in categories or some foods do not match food guide	List has less than three foods for each category or category missing	List has three or more appropriate foods for each category
Drew a healthy meal with something from each food group	Drawing is missing or incomplete	Drawing shows at least one example from two to three groups	Drawing shows at least one example from four groups	Drawing shows at least one example from each food group
Labeled each item in the meal	Labels are incorrect or missing	One or two labels are present and correct	Most items are labeled correctly	All items are labeled correctly
Wrote or told how your meal is healthy	Explanation is minimal or lacking	Connections to Food Guide are weak or incorrect	Show one connection of the meal to the Food Guide	Shows several connections of the meal to the Food Guide

INTERMEDIATE GRADE PERFORMANCE ASSESSMENT: INVESTIGATING STATES OF MATTER

Purpose: This performance task is designed to assess the student's ability to do the following:

- Conduct a scientific investigation.
- Describe properties and changes of properties in matter.
- Use appropriate tools to gather, analyze, and interpret data.
- Think critically and logically.
- Apply science concepts to natural phenomena.

Prior learning: Students should have had instruction related to the states of matter: solid, liquid, and gas. They should have conducted

(Continued)

(Continued)

investigations related to the change of state of water from solid to liquid, and from liquid to gas, used equipment and tools to collect data, constructed reasonable explanations related to data, and communicated explanations related to their findings. Students should have had experience making and recording observations and finding the mass of objects in grams.

Task: In this task, students will investigate the change of state of water from liquid to solid and make inferences related to their findings.

Management: The task may be done in small groups or individually. Students may be given a data sheet with the data table and space for predictions, observations, explanations, and so forth, or they may draw a data table and record data and explanations in their notebooks.

Materials: Provide each group or person with a small plastic cup that will hold 250 ml of water; plastic cup or 500 ml beaker, water, salt, graduated cylinder; balance and mass set or gram scale; marking pen; notebooks. Provide access to a freezer for overnight storage.

Activate and engage: Review with students what they learned about properties of matter and properties of water. Read a book about the *Titanic* and show pictures emphasizing the cause of the disaster (an iceberg) and its properties, such as the following: Titanic: *The Disaster That Shocked the World* by Mark Dubowski or *Inside the* Titanic by Hugh Brewster and Ken Marschall.

Inquiry question: What property of water in the solid state may have contributed to the *Titanic* disaster?

Acquire and explore: Student directions for Day 1: Find the mass of the empty cup and record it on the data table. Measure 250 ml of water and add this to the cup. Find the mass of the cup and water and record. Observe the level of water in the cup and make a mark on it to show the level of water. Mark the cup with your name or a symbol. Place the cup of water into the freezer.

Predict: How will the cup of water change when it is put into the freezer overnight?

Record your prediction.

Prediction: _____

_____

Day 2: Take the cup from the freezer. Find and record the mass of the cup with ice on the data table.

Record any observations you make about the cup and water.

Observations: _____

_____

DATA TABLE

Mass of cup and water	_____ grams
Mass of cup alone	_____ grams
Mass of water	_____ grams
Mass of cup and ice	_____ grams
Mass of cup alone	_____ grams
Mass of ice	_____ grams

Explain and apply: Answer these questions in your notebook

1. What did you observe about the levels of water and ice in the cup?

2. Has the mass of the cup and water changed from the liquid state to the solid state? Explain why you think it did or did not change.

3. What inference can you make about what happens to water when it changes from a liquid to a solid? That is, suggest an explanation for the change you observed.

4. Write a summary statement describing what you learned about the properties and changes of properties in matter.

Elaborate and extend: Predict: Does (fresh water) ice sink or float in salt water? Take the ice from the cup and put it into a beaker or cup of water. Add a teaspoon or so of salt and observe what happens. Describe what you see.

Based on your observation, what can you infer about how icebergs appear on the surface of water?

How much of an iceberg do you think is visible above the surface of the ocean? (about one ninth)

Apply what you learned to what happened in the story of the *Titanic.*

Research icebergs (http://en.wikipedia.org/wiki/Iceberg).

Assess and evaluate: Figure 57 identifies the objectives or indicators of learning that will be assessed through this task and suggested ways that teachers might gather evidence of student learning.

(Continued)

(Continued)

Figure 57   Objectives and Assessment Strategies

Objectives Assessed Through This Task The student will . . .	Suggested Assessment Tools and Strategies
Conduct a scientific investigation effectively	Observation checklist; quality of data table; journal entries and explanations
Use appropriate tools to gather, analyze, and interpret data	Observation checklist
Think critically and logically	Discussion; informal interview or dialog; journal entries and explanations
Describe properties and changes of properties of matter	Informal interview or dialog; data table; journal entries and explanations
Apply science concepts to natural hazards	Discussion; journal entries

CREATING RUBRICS FOR TEACHER ASSESSMENT AND SELF-ASSESSMENT

One of the greatest challenges in assessing learning through performance tasks is the ability to identify the critical knowledge and skill features of the task. Every performance task contains important underlying features or indicators of the critical dimensions of learning and inquiry.

What are they? Rubrics can be thought of as a set of criteria that provides direction in determining what students know and are able to do.

Why do we use them? In their simplest form, rubrics are nothing more than an answer key for a multiple-choice test. In this case, the only rule is to count the number of correct answers and perhaps cluster the answers into different subtest scores. The rubrics for multiple-choice, paper-and-pencil tests are simple; much more thought and consideration is required when one is developing rubrics for a rich performance task.

What do they look like? Performances, whether at the paper-and-pencil level or the activity level, can be assessed with holistic, generalized, or analytic rubrics. The criteria for assessing learning should be determined by the teacher prior to administering the test or performance task or after students have performed the task by using student "anchor" papers, that is, responses by students that provide examples of achievement levels.

Holistic Rubrics

A holistic rubric requires the teacher to think about or consider an entire task as a single entity. According to holistic experts, the focus should be on the performance, not on predesigned rubrics.

To develop holistic rubrics, teachers identify a worthy task, have students perform the task, and then view the performances in their entirety. Once teachers have viewed the performances, they separate them into two groups: those that were adequate and those that were not. Once the performances have been separated, teachers review the adequate performances and select subgroups that stood out as exceptional and those that were acceptable. Then teachers review the performances that they determined were inadequate. They once again separate the inadequate performances into two subgroups: those performances that display serious inadequacies and those that are simply inadequate.

Finally, teachers return to each of the four groups, ranging from poor to exceptional, and identify the characteristics that best describe each category or group. These descriptions constitute the final rubric which is used to score other student work on the same performance. Performances that represent the characteristics of each of the four groups can be selected and used to better clarify the different categories of the rubric.

Generalized Rubrics

Some experts contend that the disciplines are interconnected through similar dimensions and, therefore, generalized statements can be written that relate to a variety of performances within the same discipline or across disciplines. Generalized scoring rubrics provide a framework for assessing a task without explicitly identifying discrete indicators. They are used to assess concept understanding, process skills, habits of mind, and Science-Technology-Society (S-T-S) connections, and are designed by identifying indicators of learning that relate to important goals and standards. Several levels of performance are described for the performance, ranging from little understanding or ability to mastery level.

Figure 58 identifies the dimensions of a performance task in terms of the following: (a) the understanding of concepts and principles including the use of terminology, the quality and accuracy of explanations, and the quality and accuracy of representations; and (b) the skills of inquiry including the use of skills and strategies, the use of tools and technology, and the ability to make connections.

This generalized rubric consists of categorical descriptions on a continuum ranging from novice to expert. Teachers are required to select the category along the continuum that best represents the student performance.

Figure 58	A Generalized Rubric for Performance Tasks in Science			
Indicator of Learning	**Novice**	**Apprentice**	**Practitioner**	**Expert**
Understanding of Concepts and Principles				
Use of Terminology	• Little or no use of terminology • Inappropriate use to describe and explain	• Some use of terminology • Some used inappropriately	• Uses available terminology • Most used appropriately	• Uses all available terminology • All used appropriately
Explanation (Communication also assessed in inquiry section)	• Explanation or conclusion faulty or inappropriate	• Accurate explanation or conclusion with no support	• Accurate and clear explanations or conclusion with some support	• Accurate and clear explanation or conclusion with excellent support and elaboration
Representation	• Little or no use of graphic organizer(s) to organize data or show thought patterns • Inappropriate use of graphic organizer(s)	• Some attempt to use graphic organizer to show data or thought • Obvious errors	• Good use of graphic organizer(s) to show data or thought patterns • All or most used appropriately • Some error	• Excellent use of graphic organizer(s) to show data or thought patterns • All graphics labeled and used appropriately
Inquiry: The Ability to Use Process and Thinking Skills, Tools, and Technologies in a Variety of Contexts				
Use of Skills and Strategies (Includes ability to understand and do inquiry and to apply and communicate findings)	• Shows little or no evidence of use of skills or strategies • Inappropriate use of skills or strategies	• Shows some use of skills or strategies • Some used appropriately	• Shows good use of skills and strategies • Most used appropriately	• Shows excellent and appropriate use of all skills and strategies
Use of Tools and Technologies	• Shows little or no inappropriate use of tools or technologies (rulers, balances, magnifiers, models, and so forth)	• Shows some use of tools and technologies • Some used appropriately	• Shows good use of tools and technologies • All or most used appropriately	• Shows excellent and appropriate use of all tools and technologies
Making Connections	• Shows little or no connections made to technology or society • Inappropriate examples given	• Some connections made to technology or society • Some or most examples are appropriate	• Good connections of science to technology and society • All or most examples appropriate	• Excellent connections of science to technology and society • Great examples or elaboration

SOURCE: *Integrating Science With Mathematics and Literacy* (Hammerman & Musial, 2007).

Figure 59 shows another example of a generalized rubric. This rubric may be used to assess group participation.

Analytic Rubrics

Analytic rubrics are user-friendly and enhance interrater reliability. Analytic scoring is a simple and efficient way to get insight into a student's strengths and weaknesses and help diagnose problems related to a student's concept understanding, skills, or behavior. For example, in a performance task where students are asked to identify a relationship between

Figure 59   Generalized Rubric for Group Participation

	Not Yet	Needs Practice	On the Team	Team Leader
Level of Cooperation	Not active; no initiative; tasks incomplete; does not get along well with others	Takes semi-active role with little enthusiasm; tasks not complete; does not share ideas or materials; low level of cooperation	Assumes active role as team player with interest; does own share of work; mostly cooperative; tasks nearly complete or complete	Assumes active role as team leader; shares ideas with others; cooperative; displays initiative; tasks complete
Behavior in Group	Behavior disruptive; off task; negative toward others	Has little to say or offer; not helpful; works on his or her part of task; accepts little responsibility	Works with others; shares ideas when asked; positive; takes responsibility for own work; gets along	Friendly and respectful to others; accepts responsibility and offers assistance; positive and encouraging
Effort and Productivity	Effort is lacking; shows little interest; little or no productivity	Gives some attention to task; wastes time; effort inconsistent; persistence low; does not complete task	Works on task; effort mostly consistent; some persistence; tasks are complete or nearly complete	Approaches tasks with enthusiasm; effort is consistent; is persistent and thorough; tasks are completed on time

two variables, such as the effect of fertilizer on plant growth, the teacher could use the score to provide immediate feedback to students, enabling them to reconsider, continue, or replicate their experiment.

The identification of individual concepts and skills that are inherent in a task allows teachers to assess concept understanding and process skills and habits of mind as separate components. This discrete approach to developing rubrics is called analytic scoring.

For any task, the teacher decides which of the many features within the task will be assessed, since only the individual teacher (often with input from students) can determine which of the many learning opportunities inherent in the tasks are to be included and assessed through the rubric. Using the dimensions of concept understanding, concept application, thinking strategies and process skills, habits of mind, and S-T-S connections as a guide, the teacher lists student behaviors or indicators of learning that relate to the important learning dimensions and assigns a numerical "score" based on whether the work "meets" or "does not meet" the expectations of learning. In some cases, student work may "exceed expectations." Another way to show categories is to score the work as "complete" (there is sufficient evidence), "almost" (evidence present but incomplete), or "not yet" (little to no evidence).

There are times when an indicator of learning is either shown or not shown, thus assigned a numerical value of one or zero. For example, for an indicator of learning such as "the student stated a measurable hypothesis," the student either did or did not state a measurable hypothesis—there are no other choices. The score column may include "N/A" for indicators listed that do not apply to the task or to the child. A column may be shown for a "weighted score" if an indicator is thought to be more important than other indicators and thus worthy of more points.

Ideally, the levels of performance and scoring system used to assess the student performance and work should be determined by teachers with input from students, and each level and score should have meaning to both teachers and students. What is most important is to structure the rubrics to provide the most information to the students to both guide their work and to provide information about the quality of their work.

Indicators of learning that might be assessed in a performance task are shown on an analytic scoring rubric in Figure 60.

Figure 60   Analytic Scoring Rubric for a Science Investigation

Indicators of Learning The student . . .	Exceeds 2	Meets 1	Does not meet 0	Weight	Score
Made a reasonable prediction					
Made and recorded observations					
Used measurement equipment properly					
Obtained accurate data					
Collected and recorded data					
Analyzed data correctly					
Drew logical conclusion(s)					
Made appropriate type of graph or graphic					
Applied concepts to new situations					
Worked well in cooperative group					
Showed respect for equipment or living things					

PLANNING DIFFERENTIATED INSTRUCTION: THE KEY TO SUCCESS

"The person who says it cannot be done should not interrupt the person doing it."

—Chinese proverb

In Chapter 1 we identified a planning model for differentiated instruction that provides a framework for designing and implementing differentiated instruction. The step-by-step approach to planning instruction is steeped in research-based strategies for increasing student knowledge, skills, and dispositions in the context of standards-based science. Each chapter identifies and defines considerations for planning instruction and provides suggestions for strategies that address the abilities, needs, and interests of students, that is, differentiating instruction.

The planning process is one that embraces and strongly supports the latter part of the proverb:

"Give me a fish and I eat for a day. Teach me to fish and I eat for a lifetime."

Changes in ways that science is taught and learned occur when teachers develop a greater understanding of the components of and need for planning as defined in the model. Planning high quality lessons and units of instruction with the guidance and support of knowledgeable leaders provides teachers with new ways of knowing, thinking, and acting that will ultimately enrich their lives and the lives of thousands of students.

CONSIDERATIONS, RESOURCES, AND STRATEGIES FOR DIFFERENTIATING INSTRUCTION IN SCIENCE

Figure 61 shows another view of the Planning Guide. Here each section on the left-hand side of the figure identifies one of the considerations for planning differentiated instruction in science in terms of what it is and how it can be addressed. The right-hand column identifies resources and strategies for success.

Figure 61   Planning Guide for Differentiated Instruction in Science

Considerations for Planning Differentiated Instruction in Science	Resources and Strategies for Differentiating Instruction in Science
Standards and Clear Targets *What:* What students should know and be able to do to function successfully in the science and technology-based, global society. *How* • Become familiar with national, state, and local curriculum documents and goals that focus on education for the twenty-first century. • Join professional science organizations at the national and state levels.	*Resources* • National, state, and local standards documents. • Goals and standards of core curriculum areas. • Goals for information and communication technology literacy. • Professional organizations such as the National Science Teachers Association and state affiliates. *Strategies* • Become familiar with goals and standards for your grade level. • Use test scores, portfolios, and student-related data for planning instruction.
Content, Skills, and Dispositions *What:* Concepts and principles from the state and local frameworks for science education for your grade level; process and thinking skills; dispositions that are valued in science and society. *How* • Research and review content. • Select a set of key concepts based on high priority standards around which instruction will be designed. • Design instruction to address the full range of science standards using process and thinking skills and tools of technology. • Address skills of information and communication technology, practice dispositions, link learning to personal lives and to society.	*Resources* • State and local curriculum guides. • Government Web sites and reliable Internet resources. • Reference books and journals. • Videotapes and educational programs. • Informal science centers. • Community resources, content courses. *Strategies* • Identify concepts and essential questions. • Learn or review content knowledge from reputable sources. • Design a set of learning activities and experiences through which to address science standards and content, develop and apply process and thinking skills, and practice the dispositions of science. • Use a variety of methods and strategies to engage students.
Know the Learner *What:* Know learners; make data-driven decisions to accommodate student learning styles, multiple intelligences, readiness for learning, and interests. Focus on research-based effective practices. *How* • Know students; pre-assess. • Design instruction using an inquiry approach.	*Resources* National Science Foundation funded projects and programs such as Science and Technology for Children, GEMS, FOSS, and others; AIMS Activities, Delta Science Modules, National Science Teachers Association developed materials, and other reputable activity-based products. • Internet sites for universities and federally funded agencies (NASA, U.S. Geological

Figure 61 (Continued)

Considerations for Planning Differentiated Instruction in Science	Resources and Strategies for Differentiating Instruction in Science
• Plan activities, experiences, and resources for all students. • Use varied methods and strategies. • Provide choices, resources, and support for options. • Include opportunities for relearning and extended learning.	Survey, and so forth) and private organizations offering information and resources for teachers; teacher-developed inquiry-based lessons; student generated inquiries. • Videotapes, CDs, DVDs; Internet resources for students. • Field experience and community resources. • Reference books, collections, models. • Study groups, professional development books; conferences and workshops. *Strategies* • Know your students; base instruction on research-based effective practices. • Consider adjustable assignments, varied grouping patterns, cooperative learning strategies, centers, and community-based learning opportunities. • Consider individualized approaches such as student-constructed inquiries, contracts, centers, projects and products, and research.
Activate and Engage *What:* Focus attention, identify inquiry questions, motivate students, establish a relevant context. *How* • Assess prior knowledge. • Create wonder. • Ignite curiosity. • Capture attention.	*Strategies* • Begin lessons with discrepant events, high interest activities, demonstrations, quizzes, K-W-L charts, news broadcasts or journal articles, videotapes, research findings, stories, letters, or appeals relevant to the content area. • Relate topic and questions to major science-related events such as tsunamis, floods, volcanic eruption, or space exploration. • Relate topic and questions to students' lives, community issues, or environmental problems.
Acquire and Explore *What:* Whole group, small group, or individual investigations and experiences focused on inquiry (essential) questions. *How* • Research and design learning activities and experiences to address key concepts and skills.	*Resources* • Context-appropriate investigations addressing important content. • A consistent inquiry format such as the "5 E's." • Commercial products, teacher-designed units and lessons, informal science centers, Internet and community resources.

Considerations for Planning Differentiated Instruction in Science	Resources and Strategies for Differentiating Instruction in Science
• Include varied methods and strategies to meet the needs of learners. • Use a consistent format for activities. • Include the use of notebooks. • Build concept understanding from concrete to abstract. • Integrate science with math, language arts, and other areas of the curriculum. • Consider resources, equipment, and materials that will be needed for effective instruction. • Consider management strategies and safety issues.	*Strategies* • Develop lessons that include firsthand experiences, hands-on activities, demonstrations, and discussions. • Include opportunities for projects, products, and individualized learning. • Acquire reference books, videotapes, and other audiovisual and Internet resources. • Identify community resources and guest speakers. • Integrate science with reading, writing, math, thinking and problem solving, and technology. • Design student notebooks to document process and learning; include predictions, investigations, data tables, graphs, charts, diagrams, pictures, or illustrations, summary statements and conclusions, and applications.
Explain and Apply Learning; Create Meaning *What:* A variety of ways for students to reflect on and describe learning, frame thought, link new learning to prior learning, apply concepts, and make connections to their lives, technology, and society. *How* • Design questions that focus attention on processes, thinking, and concept understanding. • Design graphic organizers to show relationships between prior knowledge and new knowledge. • Provide ways for students to create meaning. • Apply concepts to personal lives of students, technology, and society through examples, research, and community involvement.	*Resources* • Carefully crafted questions to elicit explanation and discussion, and create meaning. • Data tables, charts, graphs, diagrams, pictures, and illustrations to show learning. • Graphic organizers to frame thought. *Strategies* • Reflect on learning through questions and discussion. • Analyze and graph data. • Draw conclusions based on data or support explanations with data. • Link new knowledge to prior knowledge. • Draw and describe new thinking frames. • Research applications of concepts using Internet, audiovisual, and community resources. • Explain or demonstrate applications to personal lives, technology, and society. • Generate new questions and action plans for extended learning.
Elaborate and Extend *What:* Research or investigate to answer new questions or learn more about topics of interest related to the standards.	*Resources* • Reference books, audiotapes and videotapes, movies, community and human resources, informal science centers, artifacts.

(Continued)

Figure 61 (Continued)

Considerations for Planning Differentiated Instruction in Science	Resources and Strategies for Differentiating Instruction in Science
How • Identify new questions or areas of interest. • Research information in a variety of ways. • Design an action plan. • Engage in an action research or project; create a product; visit a science center.	• Posters, models, and collections. • Computers and the Internet. *Strategies* • Interview peers, adults, community leaders, scientists, and others. • Research information using reputable Internet Web sites, reference books, videotapes, research studies, and other resources. • Trace the history of a topic or issue. • Visit government Web sites to learn about the Space Program, Human Genome Project, and other government-supported science projects. • Get involved in community-based projects. • Make a model or design a product or invention. • Research global problems and issues related to standards-based concepts.
Assess and Evaluate **What:** Evidence of student learning to inform and guide instruction and to determine what students know and are able to do. *How* • Use formative measures throughout instructional process. • Establish rubrics for peer and self-assessment. • Respect multiple ways of knowing. • Honor diversity. • Use assessment data to monitor, guide, and modify instruction.	*Resources* • Notebook entries, data sheets, reflections, and visuals such as posters, brochures, or booklets. • Products, projects, models, and collections. • Computers. • Reports or essays; poems and stories. • Teacher-made and standardized tests. *Strategies* • Discussions; written and verbal explanations. • Teacher-student dialog and interviews; peer review; self assessment. • Portfolios. • Performances, demonstrations, and PowerPoint, audiovisual, or face-to-face presentations. • Paper-and-pencil tests.

References

American Association for the Advancement of Science. (1989). *Science for all Americans*. New York: Oxford University Press.

American Association for the Advancement of Science. (1993). *Project 2061: Benchmarks for science literacy*. New York: Oxford University Press.

Armstrong, T. (1994). *Multiple intelligences in the classroom*. Alexandria, VA: Association for Supervision and Curriculum Development.

Aronson, E. (1978). *The jigsaw classroom*. Beverly Hills, CA: Sage.

Bailey, S. M. (1993). The current status of gender equity research in American schools. *Educational Psychologist, 28*(4), 321–339.

Barber, J., Bergman, L., Hosoume, K., Kopp, J., Sneider, C., & Willard, C. (1996). *Once upon a GEMS guide*. Berkeley, CA: The Lawrence Hall of Science.

Belenky, M. F., Clinchy, B. M., Goldberger, N. R., & Tarule, J. M. (1986). *Women's ways of knowing: The development of self, voice, and mind*. New York: Basic Books.

Bellanca, J., & Fogarty, R. (1991). *Blueprints for thinking in the cooperative classroom*. Thousand Oaks, CA: Corwin Press.

Bennett, B., Rolheiser-Bennett, C., & Stevahn, L. (1991). *Cooperative learning: Where heart meets mind*. Toronto, Ontario, Canada: Educational Connections.

Berte, N. (1975). *Individualizing education by learning contracts*. San Francisco: Jossey-Bass.

Black, P., & Wiliam, D. (1998). Inside the black box: Raising standards through classroom assessment. *Phi Delta Kappan, 79*(2), 139–148.

Blair, J. (2000). How teaching matters: Bringing the classroom back into discussion of teacher quality. *Education Week, 20*(8), 24.

Blanchard, K. H. (1983). *The one minute manager*. New York: Berkley.

Bloom, B. S. (Ed.). (1956). *Taxonomy of educational objectives. Handbook 1: Cognitive domain*. New York: David McKay.

Brewster, H., & Marschall, K. (1997). *Inside the* Titanic. Boston: Little, Brown.

Brooks, J., & Brooks, M. (1993). *In search of understanding: The case for constructivist classrooms*. Alexandria, VA: Association for Supervision and Curriculum Development.

Burke, K. (1993). *The mindful school: How to assess authentic learning*. Thousand Oaks, CA: Corwin Press.

Burke, K., Fogarty, R., & Belgrad, S. (1994). *The portfolio connection*. Thousand Oaks, CA: Corwin Press.

Caine, G., Caine, R. N., & Crowell, S. (1994). *Mindshifts: A brain-based process for restructuring schools and renewing education*. Tucson, AZ: Zephyr.

Caine, R. N., & Caine, G. (1991). *Making connections: Teaching and the human brain.* Alexandria, VA: Association for Supervision and Curriculum Development.

Caine, R. N., & Caine, G. (1994). *Making connections: Teaching and the human brain.* Reading, MA: Addison-Wesley.

Caine, R. N., & Caine, G. (1997). *Education on the edge of possibility.* Alexandria, VA: Association for Supervision and Curriculum Development.

Campbell, D. (1998). *The Mozart effect.* New York: Avon.

Campopiano, J., Hillen, J., Kinnear, J., Laidlaw, W., Rice, N., & Zahlis, K. (1987). *Math + science: A solution.* Fresno, CA: AIMS Education Foundation.

Cantelon, T. (1991a). *The first four weeks of cooperative learning, activities and materials.* Portland, OR: Prestige.

Cantelon, T. (1991b). *Structuring the classroom successfully for cooperative team learning.* Portland, OR: Prestige.

Cardoso, S. H. (2000). Our ancient laughing brain. *Cerebrum: The Dana Forum on Brain Science, 2*(4), 15–30.

Cawalti, G. (Ed.). (1995). *Handbook of research on improving student achievement.* Arlington, VA: Educational Research Service.

Chapman, C. (1993). *If the shoe fits: How to develop multiple intelligences in the classroom.* Thousand Oaks, CA: Corwin Press.

Chapman, C., & Freeman, L. (1996). *Multiple intelligences centers and projects.* Thousand Oaks, CA: Corwin Press.

Chapman, C., & King, R. (2000). *Test success in the brain compatible classroom.* Tucson, AZ: Zephyr.

Clarke, J., Wideman, R., & Eadie, S. (1990). *Together we learn.* Scarborough, Ontario, Canada: Prentice Hall.

Cole, D. J., Ryan, C. W., Kick, F., & Mathies, B. K. (2000). *Portfolios across the curriculum and beyond* (2nd ed.). Thousand Oaks, CA: Corwin Press.

Collins, D. (1998). *Achieving your vision of professional development.* Greensboro, NC: SERVE.

Costa, A. (1995). *Outsmarting I.Q.: The emerging science of learnable intelligence.* Old Tappan, NJ: Free Press.

Costa, A., & Garmston, R. (2002). *Cognitive coaching: A foundation for Renaissance Schools* (2nd ed.). Norwood, MA: Christopher-Gordon.

Cowan, G., & Cowan, E. (1980). *Writing.* New York: John Wiley.

Csikszentmihalyi, M. (1990). *Flow: The psychology of optimal experience.* New York: HarperCollins.

Damasio, A. R. (1999). *The feeling of what happens: Body and emotion in the making of consciousness.* New York: Harcourt Brace.

Deal, T. E., & Peterson, K. D. (1999). *Shaping school culture: The heart of leadership.* San Francisco: Jossey-Bass.

de Bono, E. (1987). *Edward de Bono's cort thinking.* Boston: Advanced Practical Thinking.

de Bono, E. (1999). *Six thinking hats.* Boston: Little, Brown.

Deporter, B., Reardon, M., & Singer-Nourie, S. (1998). *Quantum teaching.* Boston: Allyn & Bacon.

Diamond, M., & Hopson, J. (1998). *Magic trees of the mind.* New York: Penguin.

Diamond, M. C. (1967). Extensive cortical depth measurements and neuron size increases in the cortex of environmentally enriched rats. *Journal of Comparative Neurology, 131,* 357–364.

Doyle, M., & Strauss, D. (1976). *How to make meetings work.* New York: Playboy.

Driscoll, M. E. (1994, April). *School community and teacher's work in urban settings: Identifying challenges to community in the school organization.* Paper presented at the annual meeting of the American Educational Research Association, New Orleans, LA (available from New York University).

Dubowski, M. (1998). *Titanic: The disaster that shocked the world.* New York: DK Publishing, Inc.

DuFour, R., & Eaker, R. (1998). *Professional learning communities at work: Best practices for enhancing student achievement.* Bloomington, IN: National Educational Service.

Dunn, K., & Dunn, R. (1992). *Bringing out the giftedness in your child.* New York: John Wiley.

Dunn, R. (1990, Winter). Teaching underachievers through their learning style strengths. *International Education, 16*(52), 5–7.

Dunn, R., & Dunn, K. (1987). Dispelling outmoded beliefs about student learning. *Educational Leadership, 44*(6), 55–61.

Fogarty, R. (1998). *Problem-based learning and other curricular models for the multiple intelligences classroom.* Thousand Oaks, CA: Corwin Press.

Fogarty, R., & Stoehr, J. (1995). *Integrating curricula with multiple intelligences: Teams, themes and threads.* Thousand Oaks, CA: Corwin Press.

Fullan, M. (2001). *Leading in a culture of change.* San Francisco: Jossey-Bass.

Fullan, M. (with Steigelbauer, S). (1991). *The new meaning of educational change.* New York: Teachers College Press.

Gardner, H. (1983). *Frames of mind: The theory of multiple intelligences.* New York: Basic Books.

Gardner, H. (1993). *Multiple intelligences: The theory in practice.* New York: Basic Books.

Gardner, H. (1999). *Intelligence reframed: Multiple intelligences for the 21st century.* New York: Basic Books.

Gartrell, J. E., & Schafer, L. E. (1990). *Evidence of energy.* Arlington, VA: National Science Teachers Association.

Gess-Newsome, J., & Lederman, N. G. (Eds.). (1999). *Examining pedagogical content knowledge.* Dordrecht, The Netherlands: Kluwer.

Gibbs, J. (1995). *Tribes: A new way of learning and being together.* Santa Rosa, CA: Center Source.

Given, B. K. (2002). *Teaching to the brain's natural learning systems.* Alexandria, VA: Association for Supervision and Curriculum Development.

Glasser, W. (1990). *The quality school.* New York: Harper & Row.

Goleman, D. (1995). *Emotional intelligence.* New York: Bantam.

Goleman, D. (1998). *Working with emotional intelligence.* New York: Bantam.

Green, E. J., Greenough, W. T., & Schlumpf, B. E. (1983). Effects of complex or isolated environments on cortical dendrites of middle-aged rats. *Brain Research, 264,* 233–240.

Gregorc, A. (1982). *Inside styles: Beyond the basics.* Columbia, CT: Gregorc Associates.

Gregory, G. H., & Chapman, C. (2002a). *Differentiating instruction to meet the needs of all learners, elementary edition.* Sandy, UT: Teach Stream/Video Journal of Education.

Gregory, G. H., & Chapman, C. (2002b). *Differentiating instruction to meet the needs of all learners, secondary edition.* Sandy, UT: Teach Stream/Video Journal of Education.

Gregory, G. H., & Chapman, C. (2007). *Differentiated instructional strategies: One size doesn't fit all* (2nd ed.). Thousand Oaks, CA: Corwin Press.

Gregory, G. H., & Parry, T. (2006). *Designing brain-compatible learning.* Thousand Oaks, CA: Corwin Press.

Guskey, T. R. (1994). Teacher efficacy: A study of construct dimensions. *American Educational Research Journal, 31,* 627–641.

Hammerman, E. (2005). Linking classroom instruction and assessment to standardized testing. *Science Scope, 28*(4), 26–32.

Hammerman, E. (2006a). *Becoming a better science teacher: Eight steps to high quality instruction and student achievement.* Thousand Oaks, CA: Corwin Press.

Hammerman, E.(2006b). Toolkit for improving practice. *Science Scope, 30*(1), 18–23.

Hammerman, E. (2006c). *Eight essentials of inquiry-based science.* Thousand Oaks, CA: Corwin Press.

Hammerman, E., & Musial, D. (2008). *Integrating science with mathematics and literacy.* Thousand Oaks, CA: Corwin Press.

Hanson, J. R., & Silver, H. F. (1978). *Learning styles and strategies.* Moorestown, NJ: Hanson Silver Strong.

Hargreaves, S., & Fullan, M. (1998). *What's worth fighting for out there?* New York: Teachers College Press.

Harmin, M. (1994). *Inspiring active learning.* Alexandria, VA: Association for Supervision and Curriculum Development.

Harris, J. R. (1998). *The nurture assumption.* New York: Free Press.

Hart, L. A. (1998). *Human brain and human learning.* Kent, WA: Books for Educators.

Healy, J. (1992). *Endangered minds: Why our children don't think.* New York: Simon & Schuster.

Hill, S., & Hancock. J. (1993). *Reading and writing communities.* Armadale, Australia: Eleanor Curtin.

Hirsch, D. (1997). *A new vision for staff development.* Oxford, OH: National Staff Development Council.

Hofstadter, D., & Fluid Analogies Research Group. (1995). *Fluid concepts and creative analogies: Computer models of the fundamental mechanisms of thought.* New York: Basic Books.

Hord, S., Rutherford, W. L., Huling-Austin, L., & Hall, G. E. (1987). *Taking charge of change.* Alexandria, VA: Association for Supervision and Curriculum Development.

Hyerle, D. (1996). *Visual tools for constructing knowledge.* Alexandria, VA: Association for Supervision and Curriculum Development.

Institute for the Advancement of Research in Education. (2003). *Graphic organizers: A review of scientifically based research.* Portland, OR: Inspiration Software, Inc.

Jarrett, D. (1997). *Inquiry strategies for science and mathematics learning: It's just good teaching.* Unpublished document, Northwest Regional Educational Laboratory, Portland, OR.

Jensen, E. (1996). *Completing the puzzle: The brain-based approach.* Thousand Oaks, CA: Corwin Press.

Jensen, E. (1998a). *Introduction to brain-compatible learning.* Thousand Oaks, CA: Corwin Press.

Jensen, E. (1998b). *Teaching with the brain in mind.* Alexandria, VA: Association for Supervision and Curriculum Development.

Jensen, E. (2000). *Brain-based learning.* Thousand Oaks, CA: Corwin Press.

Johnson, D. W., Johnson, R. T., & Holubec, E. J. (1998). *Cooperation in the classroom.* Edina, MN: Interaction Book.

Joyce, B., & Showers, B. (1995). *Student achievement through staff development: Fundamentals of school renewal.* New York: Longman.

Kagan, S. (1992). *Cooperative learning.* San Clemente, CA: Kagan Publishing.

Kessler, R. (2000). *The soul of education: Helping students find connection, compassion, and character at school.* Alexandria, VA: Association for Supervision and Curriculum Development.

Klentschy, M., Garrison, L., & Maia Amaral, O. (2000). *Valle imperial project in science (VIPS): Four-year comparison of student achievement data, 1995–1999.* El Centro, CA: El Centro School District.

Knowles, M. (1986). *Using learning contracts.* San Francisco: Jossey-Bass.

Kohn, A. (1993). *Punished by rewards.* Boston: Houghton Mifflin.

Kolb, D. (1984). *Experiential learning: Experience as the source of learning and development.* Englewood Cliffs, NJ: Prentice Hall.

Kotulak, R. (1996). *Inside the brain: Revolutionary discoveries of how the mind works.* Kansas City, MO: Andrews & McMeel.

LeDoux, J. (1996). *The emotional brain.* New York: Simon & Schuster.

Liem, T. L. (1981). *An invitation to science inquiry.* Lexington, MA: Ginn Press.

Lost in space: Science education in New York City public schools. (2004). Unpublished report.

Lou, Y., Alorami, P. C., Spence, J. C., Paulsen, C., Chambers, B., & d'Apollonio, S. (1996). Within-class grouping: A meta-analysis. *Review of Educational Research, 66*(4), 423–458.

Lyman, F., & McTighe, J. (1988). Cueing thinking in the classroom: The promise of theory-embedded tools. *Educational Leadership, 45*(7), 18–24.

Marzano, R. J. (1992). *A different kind of classroom: Teaching with dimensions of learning.* Alexandria, VA: Association for Supervision and Curriculum Development.

Marzano, R. J., Pickering, D. J., & Pollack, J. E. (2001). *Classroom instruction that works.* Alexandria, VA: Association for Supervision and Curriculum Development.

Maslow, A. (1954). *Motivation and personality.* New York: Harper & Row.

Maslow, A. (1968). *Toward a psychology of being.* New York: Van Nostrand Reinhold.

Maurer, R. (1996). *Beyond the wall of resistance.* Austin, TX: Bard Books.

McCarthy, B. (1980). *The 4MAT system: Teaching to learning styles with right/left mode techniques.* Barrington, IL: EXCEL, Inc.

McCarthy, B. (1990). Using the 4MAT system to bring learning styles to schools. *Educational Leadership, 48*(2), 31–37.

McGee, S. B. (1993). The current status of gender equity research in American schools. *Educational Psychologist, 28,* 4, 321–339.

McLerran, A. (1985). *The mountain that loved a bird.* New York: Scholastic.

McTighe, J. (1990). *Better thinking and learning.* Baltimore: Maryland State Department of Education.

Milgram, R., Dunn, R., & Price, G. (1993). *Teaching and counseling gifted and talented adolescents.* Westport, CT: Praeger.

Miller, G. (1956). The magical number seven, plus or minus two: Some limits on our capacity for processing information. *Psychological Review, 63,* 81–97.

Moye, V. H. (1997). *Conditions that support transfer for change.* Arlington Heights, IL: IRI/SkyLight.

Multicultural education. (2003). Position paper retrieved July 30, 2007, from http://www.nameorg.org/resolutions/definition.doc

Murphy, C. U. (1997). Finding time for faculties to study together. *Journal of Staff Development, 18*(3), 29–32.

Murphy, C. U., & Lick, D. W. (1995). Whole-faculty study groups: Doing the seemingly undoable. *Journal of Staff Development, 16*(3), 37–44.

Murphy, C. U., & Lick, D. W. (2001). *Whole-faculty study groups: Creating student-based professional development.* Thousand Oaks, CA: Corwin Press.

Musial, D., & Hammerman, E. (1992). Framing knowledge through moments: A model for teaching thinking in science. *Teaching Thinking and Problem Solving, 14*(2), 12–15.

Musial, D., & Hammerman, E. (1997). *Framing ways of knowing in problem-based learning.* Unpublished manuscript.

National Research Council. (1996). *National science education standards.* Washington, DC: National Academy Press.

National Research Council. (2000). *How people learn.* Washington, DC: National Academy Press.

National Research Council. (2005). *How students learn.* Washington, DC: National Academy Press.

National Science Resources Center. (1997). *Science for all.* Washington, DC: National Academy Press.

National Science Teachers Association. (n.d.). *Gender equity in science education.* Position paper retrieved July 30, 2007, from http://www.nsta.org/about/positions/genderequity.aspx

O'Keefe, J., & Nadel, L. (1978). *The hippocampus as a cognitive map.* Oxford, UK: Clarendon.

Ornstein, R., & Thompson, R. (1984). *The amazing brain.* Boston: Houghton Mifflin.

Pardini, P. (1999). Making time for adult learning. *Journal of Staff Development, 20*(2), 37–41.

Palmer, P. (1993). *To know as we are know.* San Francisco: Harper San Francisco.

Panksepp, H. (1998). *Affective neuroscience.* New York: Oxford University Press.

Parry, T., & Gregory, G. (2003). *Designing brain-compatible learning* (2nd ed.). Thousand Oaks, CA: Corwin Press.

Pearson, C. (1992). Women as learners: Diversity and educational quality. *Journal of Developmental Education, 16*(2), 2–8, 10.

Perkins, D. (1995). *Outsmarting IQ: The emerging science of learnable intelligence.* New York: Free Press.

Pert, C. B. (1998). *Molecules of emotion.* New York: Scribner.

Peterson, L. R., & Peterson, M. J. (1959). Short-term retention of individual verbal items. *Journal of Experimental Psychology, 58,* 193–198.

Pinker, S. (1998). *How the mind works.* New York: Norton.

Purnell, S., & Hill, P. T. (1992). *Time for reform/R-4234.* Santa Monica, CA: Rand.

Reis, S., & Renzulli, J. (1992). Using curriculum compacting to challenge the above average. *Educational Leadership, 50*(2), 51–57.

Restak, R. (1993). *The brain has a mind of its own.* New York: Harmony.

Robbins, P., Gregory, G., & Herndon, L. (2000). *Thinking inside the block schedule.* Thousand Oaks, CA: Corwin Press.

Rogers, E. M. (1995). *Diffusion of innovations* (4th ed.). New York: Free Press.

Rolheiser, C., Bower, B., & Stevahn, L. (2000). *The portfolio organizer: Succeeding with portfolios in your classroom*. Alexandria, VA: Association for Supervision and Curriculum Development.

Rowe, M. B. (1986). Wait time: Slowing down may be a way of speeding up. *Journal of Teacher Education, 52,* 11.

Rozman, D. (1998, March). *Speech at Symposium on the Brain*. University of California, Berkeley.

Sadker, D. (1999). Gender equity: Still knocking at the classroom door. *Educational Leadership, 56,* 7.

Sagor, R. (1992). *How to conduct collaborative action research*. Alexandria, VA: Association for Supervision and Curriculum Development.

Samples, B., Hammond, B., & McCarthy, B. (1985). *4MAT and science: Toward wholeness in science education*. Barrington, IL: EXCEL, Inc.

Sanders, J., & Nelson, S. C. (2004). Closing gender gaps in science. *Educational Leadership, 61,* 74–77.

Sanders, W. L., & Horn, S. P. (1994). The Tennessee value-added assessment system (TVAAS): Mixed-model methodology in educational assessment. *Journal of Personnel Evaluation in Education, 8,* 299–311.

Saphier, J., & King, M. (1985). Good seeds grow in strong cultures. *Educational Leadership, 38,* 66–77.

Sapolsky, R. M. (1998). *Why zebras don't get ulcers*. New York: Freeman.

Senge, P. M. (1990). *The fifth discipline: The art and practice of the learning organization*. Garden City, NY: Doubleday.

Silvani, H. (1995). *Off the wall science: A poster series revisited*. Fresno, CA: AIMS Education Foundation.

Silver, H., Strong, R., & Perini, M. (2000). *So each may learn: Integrating learning styles and multiple intelligences*. Alexandria, VA: Association for Supervision and Curriculum Development.

Slavin, R. E. (1994). *Cooperative learning: Theory, research, and practice*. Boston: Allyn & Bacon.

Sousa, D. (2001a). *How the brain learns*. Thousand Oaks, CA: Corwin Press.

Sousa, D. (2001b). *How the special needs brain learns*. Thousand Oaks, CA: Corwin Press.

Sousa, D. (2002). *How the gifted brain learns*. Thousand Oaks, CA: Corwin Press.

Sparks, D., & Hirsh, S. (1997). *A new vision for staff development*. Oxford, OH: National Staff Development Council.

Sprenger, M. (1998). *Learning & memory: The brain in action*. Alexandria, VA: Association for Supervision and Curriculum Development.

Stepien, W., Gallagher, S., & Workman, D. (1993). Problem-based learning for traditional and interdisciplinary classrooms. *Journal for Gifted Education 16*(4), 338–357.

Sternberg, R. (1996). *Successful intelligence: How practical and creative intelligence determine success in life*. New York: Simon & Schuster.

Stiggins, R. (1993). *Student-centered classroom assessment*. Englewood Cliffs, NJ: Prentice Hall.

Sylwester, R. (1995). *A celebration of neurons: An educator's guide to the brain*. Alexandria, VA: Association for Supervision and Curriculum Development.

Sylwester, R. (2003). *A biological brain in a cultural classroom* (2nd ed.). Thousand Oaks, CA: Corwin Press.

Taba, H. (1962). *Curriculum development: Theory and practice.* Washington, DC: International Thomson.

Taba, H. (1999). *The dynamics of education: A methodology of progressive educational thought.* New York: Routledge.

Tomlinson, C. A. (1998a). *Differentiating instruction: Facilitator's guide.* Alexandria, VA: Association for Supervision and Curriculum Development.

Tomlinson, C. A. (1998b). *Differentiating instruction: Tape 2: Instructional and management strategies.* Alexandria, VA: Association for Supervision and Curriculum Development.

Tomlinson, C. A. (1999). *The differentiated classroom: Responding to the needs of all learners.* Alexandria, VA: Association for Supervision and Curriculum Development.

Tomlinson, C. A. (2001). *How to differentiate instruction in mixed-ability classrooms* (2nd ed.). Alexandria, VA: Association for Supervision and Curriculum Development.

Torp, L., & Sage, S. (1998). *Problems as possibilities.* Alexandria, VA. Association for Supervision and Curriculum Development.

U.S. Secretary of Labor. (1991). *What work requires of schools: A SCANS report for America 2000* (The Secretary's Commission on Achieving Necessary Skills). Washington, DC: U.S. Department of Labor.

Weiss, I. R., Pasley, J. D., Smith, P. S., Banilower, E. R., & Heck, D. J. (2003). *Looking inside the classroom: A study of K-12 mathematics and science education in the United States.* Chapel Hill, NC: Horizon Research, Inc.

Wenglinsky, H. (2000). *How teaching matters: Bringing the classroom back into discussions of teacher quality* [Online]. Available: http://www.ets.org/Media/Research/pdf/PICTEAMAT.pdf

Wiggins, G., & McTighe, J. (1998). *Understanding by design.* Alexandria, VA: Association for Supervision and Curriculum Development.

Winebrenner, S. (1992). *Teaching gifted kids in the regular classroom.* Minneapolis, MN: Free Spirit.

Wolfe, P. (2001). *Brain matters: Translating research into classroom practice.* Alexandria, VA: Association for Supervision and Curriculum Development.

Wolfe, P., & Sorgen, M. (1990). *Mind, memory and learning: Implications for the classroom.* Napa, CA: Authors.

Wright, R. (1994). *The moral animal.* New York: Vintage.

Wright, S. P., Horn, S. P., & Sanders, W. L. (1997). Teacher and classroom context effects on student achievement: Implications for teacher evaluation. *Journal of Personnel Evaluation in Education, 11,* 57–67.

Index

CORWIN PRESS

**Set includes a book and one
CD-ROM. Please look for both
at check-in.**

DATE DUE

OCT 1 5 2013

GAYLORD

PRINTED IN U.S.A.